CENTRAL ROCKY MOUNTAIN

Wildflowers

A FIELD GUIDE TO
COMMON WILDFLOWERS, SHRUBS,
AND TREES

H. Wayne Phillips

FALCON®

Falcon® Publishing Co., Inc., Helena and Billings, Montana

A FALCON GUIDE®

Falcon is continually expanding its list of field guides and outdoor recreational guidebooks. You can order extra copies of this book and get information and prices for other Falcon books by writing to Falcon, P.O. Box 1718, Helena, MT 59624 or calling 1-800-582-2665. Please ask for a copy of our current catalog listing all Falcon books. To contact us via e-mail, visit our home page: http://www.falconguide.com.

© 1999 by Falcon Publishing, Inc., Helena, Montana

Printed in Korea

1 2 3 4 5 6 7 8 9 0 CE 04 03 02 01 00 99

Falcon and FalconGuide are registered trademarks of Falcon Publishing, Inc.

Cover photo and all other photos by Wayne Phillips

Library of Congress Cataloging-in-Publication Data

Phillips, H. Wayne, 1941–
    Central Rocky Mountain wildflowers / Wayne Phillips.
        p.   cm. — (A Falcon guide)
    Includes bibliographical references and indexes.
    ISBN 1-56044-729-X (pbk. : alk. paper)
        1. Wild flowers—Rocky Mountains Region—Identification. 2. Wild
flowers—Rocky Mountains Region—Pictorial works. I. Title.
II. Series.
QK139.P49   1999
582.13'0978—dc21   98-46909
                                                                CIP

CAUTION

All participants in the recreational activities suggested by this book must assume responsibility for their own actions and safety. The information contained in this guidebook cannot replace sound judgment and good decision-making skills, which help reduce risk exposure; nor does the scope of this book allow for disclosure of all the potential hazards and risks involved in such activities.

Learn as much as possible about the recreational activities in which you participate, prepare for the unexpected, and be cautious. The reward will be a safer and more enjoyable experience.

CONTENTS

I dedicate this book to the memory of my mother,
Evelyn Geraldine Fields Phillips,
who encouraged me to seek my own path.

ACKNOWLEDGMENTS

I would like to thank Rick and Mary Lee Reese for getting me started in sharing my interest in wildflowers with others at the Yellowstone Institute. Much of the botanical information and many of the pictures in this book were assembled during the last fifteen years of teaching at the institute. Thanks also to all of my many students and friends at the Yellowstone Institute for their encouragement, especially Pam Gontz, Robyn Klein, Ross McCracken, and Matt Nagel.

Thanks to Bill Schneider of Falcon Publishing for inviting me to write this book and to his talented staff, especially Erin Turner and Jessica Solberg, for all of their support.

Special thanks to Kathy Lloyd and Drake Barton for editing the text, helping with the photo selection, and all the positive assurance.

To my friend Marilyn Schneider I am especially grateful. Her assistance in selecting and labeling the photos was most helpful, and her encouragement and endurance during my many long days at the word processor made the task bearable.

Thanks to Tom Kotynski, the pikas, and all of my botany and hiking friends for their encouragement, help, and patience during this project.

CENTRAL ROCKY MOUNTAIN REGION

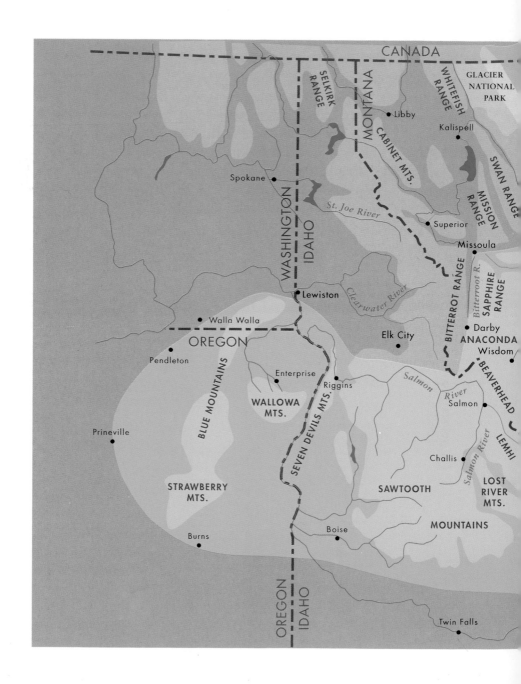

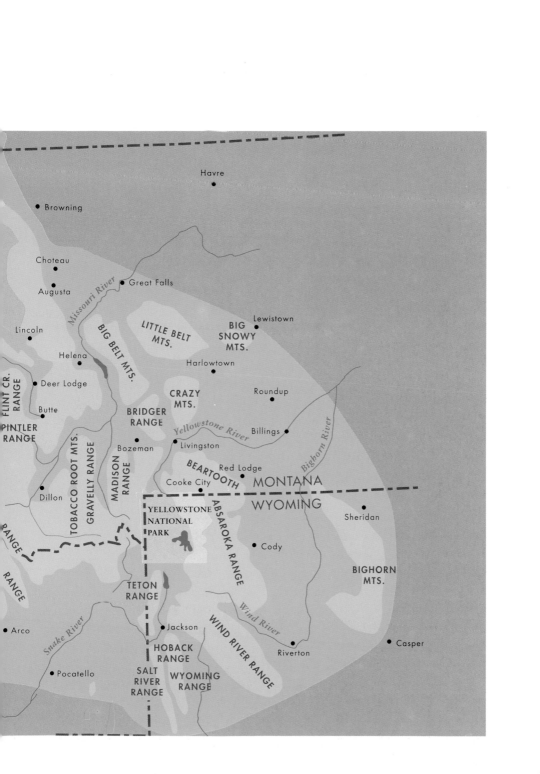

$\mathcal{J}$NTRODUCTION

The Central Rocky Mountain Region

Geography

The Central Rocky Mountains is a land of forested mountain ranges interspersed with broad, grassy valleys and plains. The region stretches from the Blue Mountains of Oregon and Washington on the western boundary to the Bighorn Mountains of Wyoming on the east, and from the Rocky Mountain front ranges of Montana on the north, to the Salt River and Wind River Ranges of Wyoming on the south. It includes more than 100,000 square miles of central and southwestern Montana, north-central and northwestern Wyoming, south-central Idaho, northeastern Oregon, and the southeastern corner of Washington.

In designating the Central Rocky Mountain region I have followed Robert G. Bailey's *Description of the Ecoregions of the United States* (1995), with two exceptions. On the north I have moved the boundary south to follow the Salmon–Clearwater watershed divide and the Bitterroot-Blackfoot Rivers. On the southeast I have moved the boundary southeast to include the Bighorn Mountains and the entire Greater Yellowstone ecosystem.

In including the whole of the Greater Yellowstone ecosystem, the Central Rocky Mountain region encompasses Yellowstone and Grand Teton National Parks. Also, the eastern fringes of Glacier and Waterton National Parks (east of the Continental Divide) are within the far northern border. In Idaho, the rugged granite spires of the Sawtooth National Recreation Area are included, as well as the National Wild, Scenic, and Recreational Salmon River. The Hells Canyon National Recreation Area, along the Snake River, cuts through the Central Rocky Mountains of Oregon and Idaho. In all, there are twenty-two national forests within the borders of the Central Rocky Mountains, from the Ochoco National Forest on the west to the Bighorn National Forest on the east, and from the Lewis and Clark National Forest on the north to the Bridger-Teton National Forest on the south. Public lands also include several hundred thousand acres of federal public land administered by the Bureau of Land Management and numerous state parks and monuments. The Wind

River Indian Reservation and portions of the Blackfeet, Crow, and Fort Hall Indian Reservations are also within the Central Rocky Mountains.

When compared with the adjacent Northern Rocky Mountains, both the valleys and mountain summits of the Central Rocky Mountains are generally higher in elevation. Elevation extremes in the Central Rocky Mountains range from below 1,000 feet in the Snake River Canyon to the 13,804-foot summit of Gannett Peak in the Wind River Range (the highest in Wyoming). The highest peaks in Idaho and Montana are also within the Central Rocky Mountains: Mount Borah in Idaho's Lost River Range (12,662 feet) and Granite Peak (12,799 feet) in Montana's Beartooth Mountains. Peaks over 11,000 feet are common in the Central Rocky Mountains within Montana's Beartooth Mountains; in the Teton, Wind River, and Absaroka Ranges of Wyoming; and in the Lost River Range and the Pioneer Mountains of Idaho. However, most mountain summits in the balance of the Central Rocky Mountains are from 8,000 to 11,000 feet in elevation and valley bottoms are typically from 3,000 to 6,000 feet in elevation.

With 5,000 feet or more of vertical relief between the valleys and summits, the Central Rocky Mountain region is a land of rugged and sharply defined mountain ranges. The region includes numerous mountain ranges both east and west of the Continental Divide in the Missouri River, Columbia River, and Green Fork of the Colorado River watersheds. The major mountain ranges within the area are listed below by state.

Idaho: Henry's Lake Mountains, Big Hole Mountains, Snake Range, Caribou Mountains, Portneuf Range, Centennial Mountains, Beaverhead Mountains, Lemhi Range, Lost River Range, White Knob Mountains, Pioneer Mountains, Boulder Mountains, White Cloud Mountains, Smoky Mountains, Sawtooth Mountains, Salmon River Mountains, Boise Mountains, Payette Crest, West Mountains, and Seven Devils Mountains.

Montana: Bighorn Mountains, Pryor Mountains, Bull Mountains, Little Snowy Mountains, Big Snowy Mountains, Judith Mountains, Moccasin Mountains, Highwood Mountains, Rocky Mountain Front Range, Big Belt Mountains, Little Belt Mountains, Castle Mountains, Crazy Mountains, Bridger Range, Beartooth Mountains, Absaroka Range, Gallatin Range, Spanish Peaks, Madison Range, Gravelly Range, Tobacco Root Mountains, Ruby Range, Snowcrest Range, Centennial Mountains, Tendoy Mountains, East and West Pioneer Mountains, Highland Mountains, Elkhorn Mountains,

Garnet Range, Flint Creek Range, Anaconda-Pintler Range, Sapphire Mountains, and Beaverhead Mountains.

Oregon: Wallowa Mountains, Blue Mountains, Strawberry Range, Ochoco Mountains, Aldrich Mountains, and Maury Mountains.

Washington: Blue Mountains.

Wyoming: Bighorn Mountains, Beartooth Mountains, Absaroka Range, Wind River Range, Gros Ventre Range, Hoback Range, Wyoming Range, Teton Range, and Salt River Range.

Climate

The Central Rocky Mountains have a temperate, semiarid climate. When compared with the more moist Northern Rocky Mountains, the Central Rocky Mountain region receives fewer days of rain and lower overall precipitation, fewer days of fog and overcast skies, more wind, and more sunny, blue-sky days, especially in the fall and winter.

The annual precipitation in the Central Rocky Mountains ranges from less than 10 inches in the drier valleys and plains to up to 60 inches on the highest mountains. Challis, Idaho, averages only 7.5 inches of precipitation. Less than 6 inches a year falls along the Clark's Fork of the Yellowstone River south of Bridger, Montana. However, precipitation in most of the valleys, plains, and foothills averages from 10 to 20 inches, while the mountainous portions of the region get from 20 to 40 inches of precipitation.

The temperate climate of the Central Rocky Mountains is continental, modified by the influence of the mountains. The region receives extreme variations in temperature between summer and winter (like the continental climate of the neighboring Great Plains), but the mountains and the warm Chinook winds modify the climate. The winter temperatures are often very cold. The coldest temperatures in both Idaho and Montana were recorded within the Central Rocky Mountains: -60°F at Island Park, Idaho, and -70°F at Roger's Pass, Montana. Summer extremes can exceed 100°F in the valleys and plains. Lewiston, Idaho, at the bottom of the Snake River Canyon, has recorded an extreme high temperature of 117°F. The average July temperature in Challis, Idaho, is 68°F, and the average January temperature is 20°F. Bozeman, Montana, is similar, with a July average temperature of 67°F and a January average temperature of 23°F.

The climate of the Central Rocky Mountains is strongly influenced by the prevailing west winds and the north-south orientation of most mountain ranges. The west slope of a mountain range usually receives more precipitation than the east slope because air masses coming from the west cool and drop moisture as they rise over the mountain range. The process is in reverse on the east side of mountain ranges, where the air masses expand, becoming warmer and drier, as they lose elevation. In the winter, these warm, downslope winds are known as Chinooks or "snow eaters." The Chinook winds of the Central Rocky Mountains modify the continental climate, causing it to be more moderate than that of the Great Plains to the east. The desirability of the warm Chinook winds of central Montana was made famous by cowboy artist Charlie Russell in his painting of a cold, raw-boned cow, entitled *Waiting for a Chinook*.

Vegetation

The vegetation of the Central Rocky Mountains is distributed in clearly defined vegetation zones (see figure 1), based on elevation and slope exposure (the cardinal direction a slope faces). At lowest elevation, the plains and mountain valleys (figure 2) support grasslands and/or sagebrush steppes (arid, treeless land supporting vegetation adapted to dry soil and extremes in temperature). Wheatgrasses, needle-and-thread grass, Idaho fescue, sagebrush, rabbitbrush, milkvetches, and many other xerophytic grasses, low shrubs, and

Figure 1. Vegetation Zones of the Central Rocky Mountains

Alpine	Cushions and turfs of moss campion, alpine forget-me-not, arctic gentian, and alpine avens
Subalpine	Forests of lodgepole pine, subalpine fir, spruce, huckleberry, arnica, and wintergreen
Montane	Forests of Douglas-fir, ponderosa pine, aspen, snowberry, pinegrass, arnica, and fairy-bells
Foothills	Open woodlands and savannahs of limber pine, ponderosa pine, juniper, fescue, balsamroot, and lupine
Plains and Valleys	Grasslands and shrublands of wheatgrasses, fescues, sagebrush, and milkvetch

Figure 2. Valleys and Plains

wildflowers are found in this driest zone. Growing along the rivers and streams are cottonwood trees, yellow willow, coyote willow, thin-leaved alder, woods rose, golden currant, and red osier dogwood.

The foothills (figure 3) lie at the base of the mountain slopes and are nearly as dry as the valleys. However, the windbreak provided by the hills and slopes results in higher moisture available for plant growth, especially on the north and east exposures. Limber pine, Rocky Mountain juniper, Douglas-fir, and ponderosa pine trees often grow in the foothills in open, widely spaced woodlands or savannahs. The vegetation under the trees is often similar to that in the valleys, with the addition of species like bitterbrush, mountain mahogany, and skunkbush sumac. Balsamroot and

Figure 3. Foothills

Figure 4. Montane

lupine are common wildflowers. Ribbons of riparian vegetation line the streams and rivers, often dominated by aspen, cottonwood, willows, red osier dogwood, golden currant, and woods rose.

Above the foothills are the forested slopes of the montane zone (figure 4). Douglas-fir and/or ponderosa pine trees often fully clothe these slopes, except on steep south and west exposures and all slopes after disturbances such as forest fires. With increasing elevation, and on cool, moist exposures, lodgepole pine and spruce become increasingly important in the forest canopy. Near the boundary with the Northern Rocky Mountains western larch and grand fir may also be found. Aspen glades and grassy parks, resplendent with wildflowers such as sticky geranium, are commonly interspersed in a mosaic pattern with the coniferous forest. Growing under the trees are a variety of low shrubs and wildflowers, including snowberry, spiraea, common juniper, ninebark, pinegrass, arnica, fairy-bells, and kinnikinnick. Spruce trees are often abundant along the streams, along with red osier dogwood, willows, aspen, and tall larkspur.

Large, continuous forests of lodgepole pine and grouse huckleberry are typical of the subalpine zone (figure 5). Subalpine fir, whitebark pine, and spruce trees form the potential climax forest in this zone, but forest fires usually occur at intervals that are too frequent (every fifty to three hundred years) for old-growth subalpine fir and spruce climax forests to

Figure 5. Subalpine

Figure 6. Alpine

fully develop. Large fires, like those in the Yellowstone National Park area and other areas of the Central Rocky Mountains in 1988, cause these areas to develop into large, even-age lodgepole pine forests. Fireweed, mountain hollyhock, and many other sun-loving flowers brighten the slopes after a fire. As the tree canopy closes, shade-tolerant plants such as arnica, meadow-rue, wintergreen, twinflower, and various huckleberry and orchid species become more abundant. The streams in the subalpine zone are often lined with spruce trees, brook saxifrage, mountain bluebells, and arrow-leaved groundsel. Wet meadows along the streams and ponds are often brilliant with blue camas, elephant's head, and monkey-flowers.

The elevation of timberline (and the other vegetation zones) varies considerably with latitude. Most mountain ranges in the Central Rocky Mountains stretch above timberline into the alpine tundra (figure 6). Along the Rocky Mountain Front Range near the northern extreme of the Central Rocky Mountains, stunted, horizontal krummholz tree growth gives way to alpine tundra at about 8000 feet of elevation, depending on exposure, while the lower timberline-prairie edge is around 4,500 to 5,000 feet. In contrast, upper timberline in the Wind River Range of Wyoming is above 10,000 feet, while trees give way to sagebrush steppes at about 7,000 feet.

Alpine tundra vegetation is generally low growing, but varies considerably in species composition, depending on exposure to the wind and available moisture. Cushion plants like alpine forget-me-not and moss campion survive in the fellfield, which is the thin, rocky soil exposed to the full blast of the high alpine winds. Where there is more soil development, turf plants like alpine avens thrive. Wetland species, such as arctic gentian, marsh-marigold, and globeflower, grow below snowbanks and along alpine streams and lakes.

Plant Characteristics

In the plant descriptions in this guide, technical botanical terms are kept to a minimum. However, knowledge of a few terms will assist the user, just as learning the names of tools makes a carpenter's work easier. Terms most often used are outlined below. Further definitions can be found in the glossary.

Life form

Is the plant woody (tree, shrub, or vine) or is it herbaceous (grass, grasslike, or forb)? (Forbs are broad-leaved, nonwoody herbaceous plants that die back to the soil surface at the end of the growing season.)

Is the plant annual, biennial, or perennial? Annual plants complete their life cycle in a single year. Biennials grow vegetatively for one year; the second year they produce seed and die. Perennials are capable of living for more than two growing seasons and usually produce seed two years or more. Trees, shrubs, and vines are always perennial. Herbaceous plants may be annual, biennial, or perennial. Most plants described in this book are perennial, herbaceous plants, unless specifically stated otherwise in the plant description.

Leaf type and arrangement (see figure 7)

Leaves may be simple or compound. A simple leaf has a single blade. This one blade may be cut or lobed, but not all the way to the midrib. A compound leaf consists of two or more blades called leaflets. Compound leaves may have their leaflets arranged palmately, ternately, or pinnately. Buds and shoots form in the axil of a leaf, but not in the axil of the leaflets of a compound leaf. The base of a leaf stalk (petiole) often has a pair of appendages called stipules. The stalk of a leaflet never has stipules. To determine if you are looking at a simple leaf, or at a leaflet of a compound leaf, look for the location of the bud and the stipules.

Figure 7. Variations of Leaf Arrangement (A), Shape (B), and Margin (C)

A. Leaf Arrangement

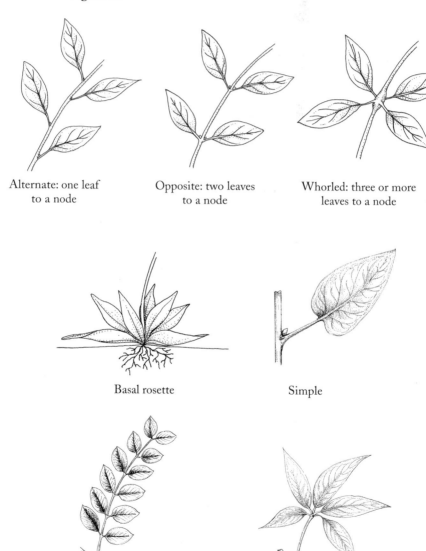

Alternate: one leaf
to a node

Opposite: two leaves
to a node

Whorled: three or more
leaves to a node

Basal rosette

Simple

Pinnately compound leaves: leaflets
arranged on both sides of the petiole

Palmately compound leaves: leaflets
spreading like fingers from the
palm of the hand

B. Leaf Shape

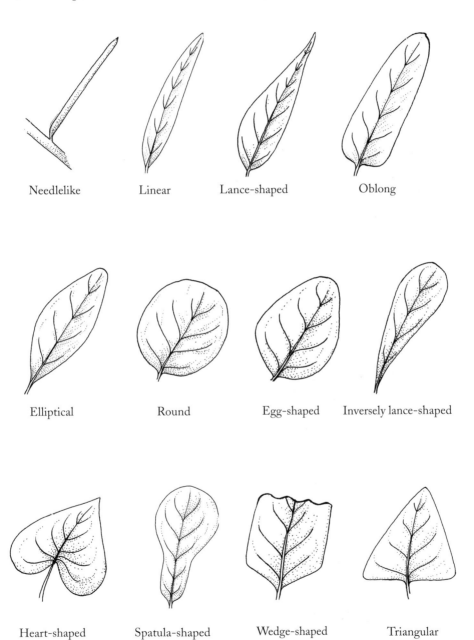

Needlelike   Linear   Lance-shaped   Oblong

Elliptical   Round   Egg-shaped   Inversely lance-shaped

Heart-shaped   Spatula-shaped   Wedge-shaped   Triangular

C. Leaf Margin

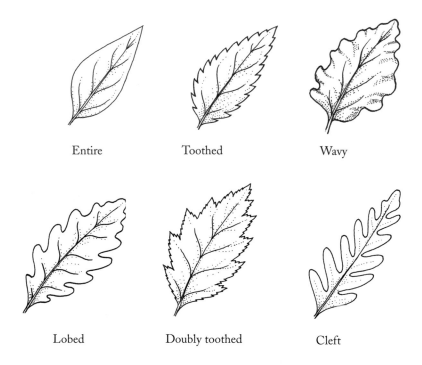

| Entire | Toothed | Wavy |

| Lobed | Doubly toothed | Cleft |

The arrangement of leaves on the stem is also important to note. Leaves may be arranged alternately on a stem, in pairs opposite each other, or whorled. Several leaves are attached to the stem at a common point in whorled leaves.

Flower arrangement or inflorescence (see figure 8)

Recognizing how the flowers are arranged on the flowering stem is often necessary in order to correctly identify a wildflower. Flowers may be solitary on the end of the stem; located in the leaf axil (axillary); or arranged in a spike, raceme, panicle, cyme, umbel, or head.

Flower parts (see figure 9)

A complete flower has floral parts arranged in four whorls. The outer whorl consists of the sepals, which are often green but may be showy and petal-like. Inside the whorl of sepals are the petals, usually the showiest part of the flower. Next are the stamens, the male part of the flower, which produce

Figure 8. Flower Arrangement or Inflorescence

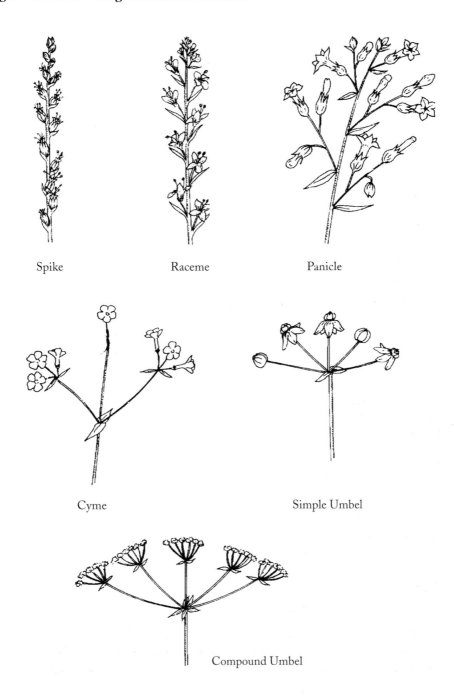

Spike   Raceme   Panicle

Cyme   Simple Umbel

Compound Umbel

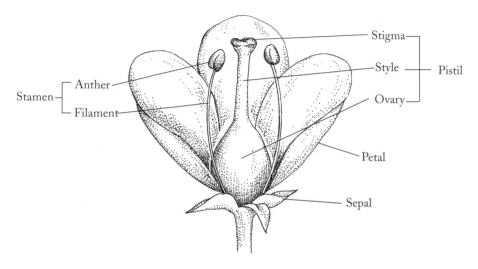

Figure 9. Typical Flower in Cross Section

the pollen. A stamen consists of a filament and an anther. Finally, in the most protected position, there is the pistil (or pistils), the female part of the flower. The pistil includes the stigma, style, and ovary. Within the ovary are the ovules, which develop into seeds after fertilization by the pollen.

Sepals and petals may be separate, or they may be united together into various shapes (tubelike, cuplike, or urnlike, etc.). Likewise, the stamens may be entirely separate or they may have their filaments or anthers joined together. For example, scarlet globemallow and other plants in the mallow family have their filaments joined together into a tube, at least on the lower portion.

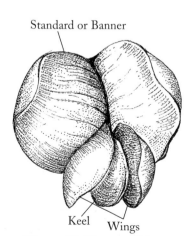

Each petal of a flower often looks much like all of the other petals. These flowers are referred to as regular. In contrast, irregular flowers have petals that are very different from one another. For example, plants in the pea family have flowers with five petals: one shaped like a banner, two shaped like wings, and the fourth and fifth petals joined together to

Figure 10. Flower of the Bean Family (Fabaceae)

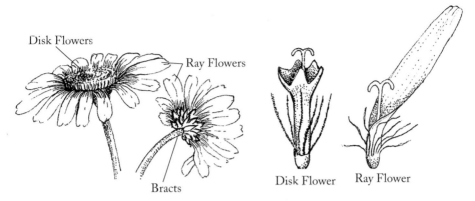

Figure 11. Flowers of the Sunflower Family (Asteraceae)

form a boatlike keel (figure 10).

When the sepals, petals, and stamens are attached at the base of the ovary, as in blue camas and other lilies, the flower is said to have a superior ovary. In contrast, an inferior ovary has the sepals, petals, and stamens attached at (or near) the top of the ovary. Fireweed and other evening primroses exhibit this characteristic.

Not all flowers are complete (with sepals, petals, stamens and a pistil). Flowers missing one or more of these parts are referred to as incomplete. Unisexual flowers are incomplete, missing either the stamens or the pistils. Other incomplete flowers may be missing either the sepals or the petals, or both. Male and female unisexual flowers are sometimes found growing on the same plant (which is described as monoecious), or they may reside on separate plants (which are referred to as dioecious).

Bracts are modified leaflike structures that lie just below the flower or flower arrangement (figure 11). In members of the aster family, the structure of the bracts is often a key feature in identification. The bracts of asters surround the base of the flower head, which is composite of many tiny flowers. The sepals of the individual flowers on the heads of asters are reduced to scales or hairlike bristles called pappus. Flowers in the aster family are found in two types, disk flowers and ray flowers. Some aster family species have flower heads with both ray and disk flowers (like sunflowers), while other species have only ray flowers (like dandelions), or only disk flowers (like pussytoes).

Using This Guide

Included in this guide are photographs and descriptions of 269 plant species from a flora of more than 2,000 species that are estimated to occur in the Central Rocky Mountain Region. I have attempted to represent most of the terrestrial plant families and a sample of the genera most likely to be encountered in the region. There are 67 plant families and 201 genera represented in this book (see index). The plants include representatives from all of the vegetation zones, from the valleys and plains to the alpine tundra. Most of the plants are common and widespread, but also included are a few rare and endemic plants of the Central Rocky Mountains. To produce an illustrated book that can be carried in the field with ease severely limits the number of species that can be included. If the species you are searching for cannot be found here, you may wish to consult the list of Selected References, which is included to further help readers in their plant study.

Flower Color

Plants are grouped in this book according to flower color: blue and purple, pink, red and orange, yellow, green, and white. Flower color is a convenient means of quickly grouping plants for identification purposes, but a word of caution is needed. Wildflowers, like all living things, are variable. No two individuals are exactly alike. Color variation is common in all plant species. For example, many white-flowered species have pale pink or lavender color variations. Also, many plants fade from white to pink or even purple as the flower ages. Some flowers even change color in response to pollination. This color change is a signal to the insect pollinator not to waste energy revisiting a flower that has already been attended to. Some plants have multicolored flowers. These plants are placed in the color group that seems most prominent.

Within each color grouping the flowers are arranged in alphabetical order by scientific name, first by the family, then the genus, and then the species. For example, all yellow aster family plants (Asteraceae) are grouped together and arranged alphabetically from *Arnica* to *Wyethia*.

Plant Names

The first name listed for each plant in this field guide is a common name. There is no universally accepted common name listing for plants. Any common name in general use for a plant in a local area is as valid as another name for the same plant in a different area. For example, serviceberry is known as sarvisberry in Montana, saskatoon in Canada, and juneberry farther East. Additional common names applied to the species are often listed in this field guide in the comments section for that species.

Carolus Linnaeus (1707–78) was the great Swedish naturalist who created the descriptive system that standardized the terminology and naming of plants and animals, and he developed a way to systematically organize the information. His system, which provides a common language for the scientific naming of organisms, has been adopted worldwide. For example, the scientific name of the bitterroot is *Lewisia rediviva,* which is a combination of *Lewisia,* the generic name, followed by the specific epithet, *rediviva.* Although there are nineteen species in the genus *Lewisia,* the binomial scientific name *Lewisia rediviva* defines only the one species that is the state flower of Montana, the bitterroot.

The scientific name is often followed by the last name (often abbreviated) of the authority who first published an account describing the species. The bitterroot first became known to the science of botany from a specimen collected by Meriwether Lewis in 1806, near present-day Missoula, Montana. The species was first described in the literature in 1814, in *Flora Americae Septentrionalis,* by Frederick Pursh. Thus, the scientific name of the bitterroot is shown as *Lewisia rediviva* Pursh in this wildflower field guide.

Although there is only one valid scientific name for a species, sometimes botanists find it necessary to change the family name or scientific name of a species. For example, if it is found that the species had been previously named in a publication that had been overlooked, the name would be changed to the earlier published name. The second name would then become a synonym or an invalid name for the species. In this field guide I have listed some of the more familiar synonyms, or currently invalid names, in parentheses as follows:

SKUNKBUSH SUMAC
Rhus aromatica Aiton
(Also *Rhus trilobata* Nutt.)
Sumac Family (Anacardiaceae)

Notice in the example above that the scientific name of the species is followed by the common name of the family, and then the scientific name of the family in parentheses. Botanists have formed the family names from the name of an included genus, followed by *-aceae.* Thus, the sumac family,

Anacardiaceae, is named for the genus *Anacardium,* which is the genus of the cashew nut of tropical America.

In a very few cases, the scientific name for a plant will include the variety. Varieties are plants that differ slightly, but consistently, from other plants within the species. They are usually found within distinct geographic ranges within that of the species as a whole. In most cases I have not described the many varieties of plant species. The user is reminded, when using the description and photograph to identify a plant, that many species have wide variations in plant characteristics.

In assigning a family and scientific name to the plants in this book I have attempted to use the most recently accepted names. In doing so I have consulted the following floral manuals: *Flora of the Pacific Northwest* (Hitchcock and Cronquist, 1973), *Flora of the Great Plains* (Barkley, 1986), *Vascular Plants of Montana* (Dorn, 1984), *Vascular Plants of Wyoming* (Dorn, 1992), *Flora of Idaho* (Davis, 1952), *Intermountain Flora* vols. 1, 3A, 3B, 4, 5, 6 (Cronquist et al., 1972), and *Flora of North America* vols. 1, 2, 3 (Morin, 1993). For more sources of information, see the Selected References.

Description

In the description section, key characteristics of each plant are provided to help the reader with identification. The unique features of the plant, including its leaves, bracts, flowers, and sometimes the fruit are described. The dimensions of the leaves and flowers are given in inches. Please note that these measurements are averages. Since plants are variable in all of their features, measurements should be taken of a number of representatives, then averaged, before deciding if the plant fits within the range given. A hand lens is sometimes necessary to see some of the tiny plant parts described in this section.

These descriptions are necessarily brief and incomplete, and they are intended to be combined with the photograph to identify the plant. Closely related plants are often also described to help the reader. There may be occasions when a plant does not exactly match an entry, though it is close. In many cases this will be because the plant in question is of a different species in the same genus as the plant that is photographed and described. Botanical manuals listed in the Selected References section may be required to resolve these identification problems. These manuals include more complete botanical keys, descriptions, and often fine line drawings of all of the species in the Central

Rocky Mountains. These manuals are readily available through the public library in most communities.

The blooming period is given at the end of the description section in italics, for example: *July–September*. This means that this species can be found blooming someplace within the Central Rocky Mountains during this period. In any one area the blooming period may be much shorter, sometimes only a week or two. Blooming and other phenological events, such as leafing out and fruit ripening, differ according to the latitude and elevation in which the plant is growing. Most of us have noticed the flowers of any given species blooming later higher in the mountains than they do in the foothills. According to A. D. Hopkins's bioclimatic law, blooming (and other spring-summer events) occurs four days later for each degree of latitude northward or 400 feet of altitude, that is, later northward and/or upward. This assumes that other habitat variables are equal, such as slope exposure. With autumn events, such as leaf color change, the sequence is reversed, with fall colors showing earlier at higher elevations and more northern latitudes. Life activity in the arctic or alpine is thus compressed into a very short period of 6 to 8 weeks.

Habitat/Range

This section describes the characteristic environment and geographic range of the plant species. Some plants found in the Central Rocky Mountains also grow in suitable habitats around the world. Others are unique to the Central Rocky Mountains, occurring nowhere else.

Plants in this book are native to the Central Rocky Mountains, unless specifically stated otherwise. Introduced species usually include those imported from Europe and Asia that have escaped cultivation or have entered accidentally and are now found growing in disturbed or undisturbed habitats in the Central Rocky Mountains. Some introduced species are native to other geographic regions of North America but have only been established in the Central Rocky Mountains since European settlement of this continent. Information about the conservation of the native wildflowers of the Central Rocky Mountains is available from the Native Plant Societies of Montana, Wyoming, Idaho, Oregon, and Washington, as well as from the Natural Heritage Database Center of each state, as listed in this book in the Native Plant Directory.

Comments

This section explains the origin of the names, the history of the discovery of the species, and/or the traditional or historical uses of the plant for food or medicine. This information is included solely to help the reader learn the plant species through association with interesting information about the plant.

This book, or any book, does not contain enough information to enable the reader to safely experiment with using plants for food or medicine. In 1984, six out of eight men on a float trip on the Owyhee River in eastern Oregon were poisoned after eating what they thought to be a wild parsnip. One of them died. In 1985, a hiker in Yellowstone National Park who used a plant guidebook to identify edible plants died a painful death from water hemlock poisoning. Please heed this warning.

In addition to posing possible health hazards, picking wildflowers and harvesting plants reduces the reproductive capacity of the native species and also the enjoyment of those who follow. The large-scale commercial harvesting ("wildcrafting") of wild medicinal plants for the skyrocketing herb market is reducing populations of certain native species of plants today in the Central Rocky Mountains and the adjacent Great Plains. Please practice "leave no trace" wildflower study. Leave the plants as you found them for others to enjoy.

WARNING

Ingesting plants or plant parts poses an extreme human health hazard, and could result in sickness or even death. No one should attempt to use any wild plant for food or medicine without adequate training by a fully qualified professional. The author, publisher, and all others associated with the production and distribution of this book assume no liability for the actions of the reader.

BLUE AND PURPLE FLOWERS

Lewis' Monkey-Flower

*This section includes flowers ranging from pale blue
to deep indigo and from lavender to violet. Since
lavender flowers grade into pink, you should check
the pink section if you do not find the flower you are
looking for here. Some purplish brown flowers,
included here, are more brown than purple.*

Alpine Aster

ALPINE ASTER
Aster alpigenus (T. & G.) A. Gray
Aster Family (Asteraceae)

Description: This purple aster is distinguished from other asters by a combination of its alpine habitat, small size, solitary heads (only one per stem), and long, linear leaves arising from the base of the plant. Only a few very small leaves occur on the flowering stem. The outer row of petals of the ray flowers are purple to lavender. The yellow disk in the center of the head consists of many tiny, 5-petaled individual flowers. This perennial aster forms a vertical taproot. Like most alpine plants, alpine asters are low, ground-hugging plants, less than 6" tall.

July–early September.

Habitat/Range: Alpine, subalpine.

Comments: *Aster* is a Greek word meaning "a star," which the flowers often resemble. *Alpigenus* refers to the Alps or the alpine habitat typical of this plant.

THICK-STEMMED ASTER
Aster intregrifolius Nutt.
Aster Family (Asteraceae)

Description: This aster has many flower heads on each flowering stem. The upper stems, foliage, and floral bracts are covered with glandular hairs. The leaves are ½–1¾" broad, with the larger ones clustered near the base of the plant; the leaves become progressively smaller up the stem. The margin of the leaf is entire, without any teeth. The whole plant is rather thick-stemmed and stout, and 6–28" tall. The flower heads have deep violet-purple ray flowers surrounding a golden yellow disk.

Late July–September.

Habitat/Range: Subalpine, montane.

Comments: Some species of aster are good forage plants for elk, deer, and other wild ungulates, especially Lindley aster (*A. ciliolatus*). However, the glandular hairs of thick-stemmed aster tend to discourage the grazing animals and defend the foliage from insects, which are often captured in the sticky fluid that exudes from the glands.

Thick-Stemmed Aster

ELEGANT ASTER
Aster perelegans A. Nels. & J. Macbr.
Aster Family (Asteraceae)

Description: Elegant aster is 1–3' tall with many flower heads on each flowering stem. The leaves are narrow (¼–½" wide) and better developed in the middle and upper part of the stem. The lower leaves on the stem become progressively smaller and tend to dry up by the time the blossoms appear. Look closely at the tiny overlapping bracts around the base of the flower heads: They are purple on the sharply pointed tip and margins and down the keeled center of each bract. The petal-like ray flowers are deep violet surrounding a golden yellow disk.

Late July–September.

Habitat/Range: Foothills, coniferous forests.

Comments: Asters usually have several series of bracts that overlap in the vertical plane, like shingles on the roof of a house. Daisies have only 1 or 2 sets of these bracts.

Elegant Aster

Showy Fleabane Daisy

SHOWY FLEABANE DAISY
Erigeron speciosus (Lindl.) DC.
Aster Family (Asteraceae)

Description: Showy fleabane is distinguished from other perennial fleabanes by its entire leaves (not lobed or toothed) that are well distributed along the full length of the stem. There is no hair on the leaves, except for a sparse fringe along the leaf margin, which is visible under a hand lens. There are 1–13 flower heads on each flowering stem. Each flower head has but a single row of narrow green bracts of equal length, and numerous blue/lavender petal-like ray flowers surrounding a golden yellow disk.

June–early August.

Habitat/Range: Foothills, subalpine, alpine.

Comments: *Erigeron* comes from the Greek *eri,* meaning "early," and *geron,* meaning "old man," named presumably because of the early flowering and fruiting habit of fleabane daisy. Some Native Americans used species of fleabane daisy for an astringent herb by boiling the root to make a strong tea. The cooled tea was used as an eyewash and to treat diarrhea or childbirth hemorrhage.

BLAZING STAR
Liatris punctata Hook.
Aster Family (Asteraceae)

Blazing Star

Description: The bright purple flower heads are arranged in spikelike groups on the end of an unbranched stem. Each individual flower head has 4–6 small purple disk flowers with 5 tiny petals each. The vertical underground stem has one or more bulblike solid swellings, or corms, for food storage. The leaves are entire, up to 5" long, less than ¼" wide, and are covered with tiny glandular dots that are visible when held up to the light. The plant is 4–16" tall.

July–September.

Habitat/Range: Plains, foothills, montane forests east of the Continental Divide.

Comments: Other common names for this plant include dotted gayfeather and button snakeroot. The Blackfeet name translates to "crow-root." The root of this plant was valued by Native American people for both food and medicine, especially for treating kidney and bladder problems and venereal disease. Herbalists today also use the root as a diuretic and mild kidney and liver tonic.

MOUNTAIN TOWNSENDIA
Townsendia montana M. E. Jones
(Also *Townsendia alpigena* Piper)
Aster Family (Asteraceae)

Description: Townsendias have a taproot, leaves that are often all basal, and flower bracts with a distinct fringe along the margin (when viewed with a hand lens). Mountain townsendia, like many others in the genus, grows close to the surface of the ground. A short flowering stem, blue-violet ray flowers, hairless seeds, and leaves that are broad and round at the tip distinguish mountain townsendia from the common townsendia (*T. leptotes*) and other low-growing species.

July–August.

Habitat/Range: Alpine; WY, southern MT, central ID, central UT, west to the Wallowa Mountains of OR.

Comments: *Townsendia* is named for David Townsend, who was an amateur botanist from Pennsylvania in the early 1800s.

Mountain Townsendia

PARRY'S TOWNSENDIA
Townsendia parryi Eat.
Aster Family (Asteraceae)

Description: Parry's townsendia has an erect stem up to 12" tall. The flower heads are huge, from 1½–3½" in diameter from the tips of the colorful ray flowers across the center of the head. The flowers are lavender to purplish or blue, and very showy. Most leaves are basal and broadened toward the tip, tapering toward the base. Leaves on the flowering stem are usually progressively smaller up the stem.

June–August.

Habitat/Range: Forest openings at intermediate and upper elevations.

Comments: Parry's townsendia was named for Charles C. Parry (1823–1890), a native of England who came to America in 1832 and contributed much to our knowledge of the native flora. He was a botanist with the Mexican Boundary Survery.

Parry's Townsendia

Pale Alpine Forget-Me-Not

PALE ALPINE FORGET-ME-NOT
Eritrichium nanum (Vill.) Schrad.
Borage Family (Boraginaceae)

Description: This alpine cushion plant grows in dense mats of basal leaves, which have a pale green color. The leaves have long, woolly hairs that are more numerous toward the leaf tip, forming a terminal tuft. The flowering stems are sometimes up to 4" tall but are often much shorter, scarcely exceeding the leaves. The flowers are deep blue to pale blue, with a bright yellow "eye." The fruit is a nutlet without prickles.

July–August.

Habitat/Range: Alpine fellfield.

Comments: The word *Eritrichium* comes from Greek roots meaning "wool" and "hair," in reference to the woolly hairs of this species. *Nanum* means "very small" or "dwarf," a good description of the size of this and other alpine fellfield cushion plants.

Many-Flowered Stickseed

MANY-FLOWERED STICKSEED
Hackelia floribunda (Lehm.) Johnst.
Borage Family (Boraginaceae)

Description: Many-flowered stickseed has blue flowers and is distinguished by having flower stalks that turn downward as the prickly nutlet fruit forms after flowering. Many-flowered stickseed is a tall, robust plant 1–3' tall. It has a single, or few, flowering stems arising from a taproot. It is a short-lived plant, often completing its life cycle in 2 years.

June–August.

Habitat/Range: Moist meadows and stream banks, foothills to subalpine.

Comments: The plant is called "stickseed" because of the prickles on the nutlets that stick to animal hair, socks, and almost anything else. In this way the seeds are carried to new places to germinate and propagate the species.

STREAMSIDE BLUEBELLS
Mertensia ciliata (Torr.) G. Don
Borage Family (Boraginaceae)

Description: Bluebells have long, tubelike blue (or pink) petals that extend well beyond the green sepals. This species is a tall, robust plant from less than 1' to as much as 5' tall. The middle and upper leaves of the flowering stems are up to 2" wide, mostly without a leaf stem (petiole), and are tapered toward the base. Several other closely related bluebell species inhabit the Central Rocky Mountains, including mountain bluebells (*Mertensia oblongifolia*), which is a smaller plant (16" high or less) that grows in grasslands and dry forests.

June–August.

Habitat/Range: Foothills, montane, subalpine.

Comments: The tender, fresh leaves and flowers of bluebells are edible fresh or cooked, and the taste is said to be like oysters. They should not be consumed in large quantities, though, because of possible toxic properties.

Streamside Bluebells

WOODS FORGET-ME-NOT
Myosotis sylvatica Hoffm.
Borage Family (Boraginaceae)

Description: Woods forget-me-not has blue flowers with a yellow "eye" that strongly resemble alpine forget-me-not (*Eritrichium*) and stickseeds (*Hackelia* and *Lappula*). However, woods forget-me-not does not form dense leafy cushions like alpine forget-me-not, and it has smooth nutlet fruits without the prickles of stickseeds. Woods forget-me-not plants are 2–16" tall. They are covered with hair that often has tiny hooks.

July–August.

Habitat/Range: Moist meadows, alpine to montane forests at moderate elevations.

Comments: *Myosotis* means "mouse ear" in Greek, probably because of the hairy mouse-ear-like appearance of the leaves. *Sylvatica* comes from the Latin component *sylv-*, referring to its sylvan (woodland or forest) habitat. It is the floral emblem of Alaska.

Woods Forget-Me-Not

Harebell

HAREBELL
Campanula rotundifolia L.
Harebell Family (Campanulaceae)

Description: Harebell has blue to white, bell-shaped flowers. There are usually several (up to 20) flowers per plant, but occasionally they are borne singly. The leaves on the flowering stem are long and less than ¼" wide. The basal leaves are broader, round to heart-shaped, but these often dry up by the time the plants are in full flower. The leaves exude a milky juice when broken. The fruit is a capsule that hangs downward and opens by pores near the base.

June–September.

Habitat/Range: Low elevations to subalpine forests.

Comments: Harebell is easy to cultivate and seeds freely. However, it can become weedy in the garden. It is also called "bluebell," but it is not related to bluebells of the genus *Mertensia* in the borage family. A closely related species, creeping bellflower (*Campanula rapunculoides*), was imported from Europe as a garden flower. This exotic relative of harebell has spread into lawns, where it is difficult to control.

MOUNTAIN-LOVER
Pachistima myrsinites (Pursh) Raf.
Staff-Tree Family (Celastraceae)

Mountain-Lover

Description: Mountain-lover is a low shrub, usually less than 2' tall. The glossy, evergreen leaves are arranged in pairs opposite each other on the stems. The leaves have fine teeth along the margin. The shiny evergreen leaves could be mistaken for those of kinnikinnick or twinflower. However, kinnikinnick has leaves that are arranged alternately and are smooth on the margin, and twinflower has a pair of showy white to pink flowers. Mountain-lover flowers are small and inconspicuous, but have 4 lovely, maroon petals.

May–June.

Habitat/Range: Montane, subalpine.

Comments: Mountain-lover is a fine ornamental shrub, being shade tolerant and easily grown. *Pachistima* comes from Greek roots meaning "thick stigma." This genus name is sometimes spelled *Paxistima* or *Pachystima*. *Myrsinites* comes from the Greek word for myrrh, which the aroma of the flowers resembles.

RED MOUNTAIN-HEATHER
Phyllodoce empetriformis (Sw.) D. Don
Heath Family (Ericaceae)

Description: Red mountain-heather is a low shrub with red bell-shaped flowers protruding from near the tips of the low branches. The closely spaced evergreen leaves resemble the needles of a fir tree. The similar moss-heather (*Cassiope* species), which is also found in the Central Rocky Mountains, has 4-ranked scale-like leaves and white flowers. The closely related yellow mountain-heather (*P. glanduliflora*) has yellow to greenish white urn-shaped flowers and sepals with glandular hairs. Red and yellow mountain-heathers are often found together and hybridize, producing offspring with pale pink flowers.

July–August.

Habitat/Range: Alpine, subalpine.

Comments: *Phyllodoce* is from the Greek name for a sea nymph. It is called "heather" because it resembles the true heather (*Calluna*) of Scotland and other European countries.

Red Mountain-Heather

THISTLE MILKVETCH
Astragalus kentrophyta A. Gray
Bean Family (Fabaceae)

Description: Thistle milkvetch is easily separated from the numerous other milkvetch species in the Central Rocky Mountains by its ground-hugging, cushion-forming growth habit; the sharp spines on the tip of the 3–9 narrow leaflets; and the groups of 1–3 small purple flowers. Like other flowers in the bean family, the petals are irregular and are differentiated into banner, wings, and keel.

June–September.

Habitat/Range: Alpine, plains.

Comments: This plant is called thistle milkvetch because of the thistlelike spines on the ends of the leaves. It is also known as cushion milkvetch because of its compact, cushionlike growth form. This belly-plant is worth getting prone for a closer look.

Thistle Milkvetch

Western Sweetvetch

WESTERN SWEETVETCH
Hedysarum occidentale Greene
Bean Family (Fabaceae)

Description: Western sweetvetch is a perennial, herbaceous plant with rose-pink to magenta-purple "bean flowers" that droop downward from 1 side of the main flower stalk. Leaves are pinnately compound, consisting of many leaflets arranged "featherlike" on either side of the main leaf axis. Sweetvetch is easily distinguished from milkvetch by having wing petals that are much shorter than the keel petal and by having fruit pods that are constricted between the seeds. The large pods of western sweetvetch have a thin, membranous margin or wing, which helps to separate this species from the similarly colored northern sweetvetch (*H. boreale*) and alpine sweetvetch (*H. alpinum*).

June–August.

Habitat/Range: Montane, subalpine.

Comments: The name *Hedysarum* is derived from the Greek *hedy* (sweet) and *saron* (broom). Sweetvetches are good forage plants for both wild and domestic animals.

Silvery Lupine

SILVERY LUPINE
Lupinus argenteus Pursh
Bean Family (Fabaceae)

Description: Lupine has flowers characteristic of the bean family, with irregular petals differentiated into banner, wings, and keel. Lupines have palmately compound leaves, and a raceme flower arrangement.

May–July.

Habitat/Range: Foothills, montane, subalpine.

Comments: *Lupine* is derived from the Latin *lupus* (wolf). *Argenteus* is from the Greek *argyr* (silver), probably because of the silvery sheen to the leaves in certain light. Silvery lupine was first described to Western science by Frederick Pursh from a specimen collected by Meriwether Lewis in the upper Blackfoot River drainage of Montana on July 7, 1806. Lupines have poisonous alkaloids concentrated in their seeds.

DWARF CLOVER
Trifolium nanum Torr.
Bean Family (Fabaceae)

Description: The trifoliate leaves of dwarf clover crowd together in dense mats about 1" or less from the ground surface. The flowering heads have only 1–4 flowers each and extend upward from the leaf mat, each flower seemingly independent of the next. Other species of clover in the Central Rocky Mountains are taller (more than 1" high) and have more than four flowers in dense heads.

June–August.

Habitat/Range: Alpine, subalpine.

Comments: Dwarf clover is also known as tundra clover. It often occurs with Parry's clover (*T. parryi*) and/or whip-root clover (*T. dasyphyllum*). All of these alpine clovers are good forage plants for mountain goats, bighorn sheep, and pikas, which share their alpine habitat.

Dwarf Clover

AMERICAN VETCH
Vicia americana Muhl.
Bean Family (Fabaceae)

Description: True vetches (*Vicia* species) are herbaceous vines with pinnately compound leaves. The leaf has a slender coiling or twining tendril on the end, which is used for climbing and grasping for support. Sweet peas (*Lathyrus* species) also have leaves with tendrils. However, a careful look at the flowers with a hand lens will show true vetches to be equally hairy all around the end of the style, while sweet peas have hair only on the inner, flattened style surface. The blue flowers of American vetch are rather large (½" long or more) and are arranged in groups of 4–10.

May–August.

Habitat/Range: Foothills to subalpine.

Comments: Like other members of the bean family, the roots of vetches have nodules that house bacterial colonies in a symbiotic relation-

American Vetch

ship. The bacteria take elemental nitrogen from the air and incorporate it into compounds that dissolve in water, making the nitrogen usable for plant growth.

EXPLORER'S GENTIAN
Gentiana calycosa Griseb.
Gentian Family (Gentianaceae)

Explorer's Gentian

Description: Explorer's gentian is a perennial, herbaceous plant with opposite, entire leaves. All leaves are on the stem (none are basal). The flowers are funnel-shaped, deep blue, and large (about 1½" long), with 5 lobes when fully opened. Before opening, the upper petal tube has a lovely pointed, spiral form, like a swirled ice cream cone. The lobes of the flower petals have conspicuous pleats between each lobe. The leaves are more or less egg-shaped, widest near the base. The leaves, stems, and sepals are smooth, without any hairs. Plant stems are usually unbranched with a single flower on the end or sometimes with a compact, few-flowered cluster.

July–early September.

Habitat/Range: Wet meadows and along stream banks in subalpine forests to the alpine.

Comments: *Gentiana* was named in honor of King Gentius of Illyria in the Adriatic, who is credited with discovering its medicinal properties. Gentians have been used for centuries as a bitter herb to improve digestion.

Smaller Fringed Gentian

SMALLER FRINGED GENTIAN
Gentianopsis detonsa (Rottb.) Ma.
(Also *Gentiana detonsa* Rottb.)
(Also *Gentiana thermalis* Kuntze)
Gentian Family (Gentianaceae)

Description: Smaller fringed gentian is an annual, herbaceous plant with opposite, narrow leaves and blue flowers borne on the end of stalks 1–6" long. The lobes of the tubular flowers are fringed along the margin and lack the pleats between the lobes that explorer's gentian and others in the genus *Gentiana* have. The green sepal lobes are prominently keeled, like a boat. The keel is often purple tinged.

Late July–September.

Habitat/Range: Wet meadows and along stream banks in the montane and subalpine forests.

Comments: This is the official flower of Yellowstone National Park, where it is common along warm streams and wet meadows in the geyser basins.

BOG SWERTIA
Swertia perennis L.
Gentian Family (Gentianaceae)

Description: Bog swertia is a perennial, herbaceous plant with a cluster of basal leaves with petioles (leaf stalks), and a few leaves attached directly to the flowering stem without petioles. The flowers have 5 purple petals and 5 green sepals. The flowers are wheel-shaped and flat, with a very short tube. Two fringed nectary glands occur near the base of each petal. The purple petals are streaked with white or green.

July–early September.

Habitat/Range: Wet meadows, in bogs, and along streams in the mountains in the subalpine forest zone.

Comments: *Swertia* is named in honor of Emmanuel Sweerts, a sixteenth-century Dutch gardener and engraver. It is often found growing in association with bog orchids.

Bog Swertia

STICKY GERANIUM
Geranium viscosissimum Fisch. &
Mey. ex Mey.
Geranium Family (Geraniaceae)

Description: Sticky geranium is a perennial, herbaceous plant with a thick, woody taproot. Petal color varies from pink to lavender or violet, with dark red veins. The leaves are deeply parted into 5–7 coarsely toothed segments. Glandular hairs cover the sepals and often the leaf stems and other parts of the plant. When touched, the glands exude a sticky, aromatic substance with a strong "geranium bouquet."

June–August.

Habitat/Range: Foothills to subalpine.

Comments: *Geranium* comes from a Greek word meaning "crane," in reference to the long, cranelike style or persistent beak of the pods. Crane's-bill is another common name for plants in the genus. Herbalists use the astringent herb to treat many conditions.

Sticky Geranium

Silky Phacelia

SILKY PHACELIA
Phacelia sericea (Grah.) Gray
Waterleaf Family (Hydrophyllaceae)

Description: Silky phacelia is a perennial, herbaceous plant having leaves deeply divided into many segments, covered with silky hairs, and with a taproot. The numerous purple to blue flowers are arranged in clusters of coiled branches, like scorpion tails, that uncoil as blooming progresses. Individual flowers have stamens with long filaments that extend well beyond the petals.

June–August.

Habitat/Range: Open, rocky slopes at moderate to high elevations in the mountains.

Comments: *Phacelia* comes from the Greek word *phakelos,* which refers to the dense flower arrangement. The plants make attractive ornamentals for the rock garden and are easily grown from seed. Some species of *Phacelia* are reported to irritate the skin when handled.

MISSOURI IRIS
Iris missouriensis Nutt.
Iris Family (Iridaceae)

Missouri Iris

Description: Missouri iris has parallel-veined leaves and flower parts in threes; an inferior ovary (floral parts attached to the top) and petal-like style branches. It has thick underground stems (rhizomes). This is the only native iris in the Central Rocky Mountains. However, a yellow-flowered domestic iris (*Iris pseudacorus*) has escaped cultivation along low-elevation streams and lakes. The large (greater than 2" long) blue flowers of Missouri iris are a common sight in low-lying areas of the Central Rocky Mountains. *May–July.*

Habitat/Range: Moist meadows from foothills to subalpine forest.

Comments: The word *iris* is Greek for "rainbow," referring to the many colors of iris flowers. Iris, or fleur-de-lis, is the national flower and emblem of France and the state flower of Tennessee. It is also often called blue flag. Iris is both a dangerous poisonous plant and valuable medicinal herb.

MONTANA BLUE-EYED GRASS
Sisyrinchium montanum Greene
(Also *Sisyrinchium angustifolium* Mill.)
Iris Family (Iridaceae)

Description: Like iris, the leaves of blue-eyed grass are folded together lengthwise in 2 ranks and are mostly basal. However, unlike iris, the petals and sepals of blue-eyed grass are short (less than 1¼" long) and similar in shape, and the style branches are not petal-like. The leaves are long and narrow, like grass leaves, but stiffer. The flowers are blue to purple with a yellow center and a bristle tip on each petal. Montana blue-eyed grass can be distinguished from the similar Idaho blue-eyed grass (*S. idahoense*) by looking at the pair of green, leaflike bracts just below the flower. The outer flower bract of Montana blue-eyed grass is nearly twice the length of the inner one.

April–July.

Habitat/Range: Meadows, moist grassy areas, and stream banks from valleys to montane.

Comments: Other names for blue-eyed grass

Montana Blue-Eyed Grass

include eyebright, grass-widows, and blue star. Rocky mountain plants were previously referred to as *S. angustifolium,* which is now recognized as an eastern species.

SMOOTH WOODRUSH
Luzula glabrata (Hoppe) Desv.
(Also *Luzula hitchcockii* Hamet-Ahti)
Rush Family (Juncaceae)

Description: The shiny green leaves of woodrush look much like those of a grass. However, the leaves of woodrush are fringed with slender hair, and the stems are round and solid. Grass leaves often do not have hair on the margin, and the round stems are usually hollow and jointed. The flowers of woodrush are lilylike in structure, although they are tiny and not at all showy. A woodrush flower has 6 similar floral segments (3 sepals and 3 petals), 6 stamens, and a pistil with 3 styles. The sepals and petals of smooth woodrush are purplish brown. The anthers are much longer than the filaments. The flowers are arranged in an open panicle; the fruit is a purplish brown capsule with 3 seeds.

July–September.

Smooth Woodrush

Habitat/Range: Cool, moist subalpine forest, often extending up into the alpine zone.

Comments: On the cool north- and east-facing slopes, up near timberline, smooth woodrush often forms large patches of lovely, pale green turf. Interspersed with it are equally dense patches of the low grouse huckleberry. The whitebark pine, spruce, and subalpine fir trees here are often widely spaced, creating a parklike forest, where the only sounds to be heard are the wing beats and raucous cries of the Clark's nutcracker.

Field Mint

FIELD MINT
Mentha arvensis L.
(Also *Mentha canadensis* L.)
Mint Family (Lamiaceae)

Description: Field mint is an aromatic herb with square stems and opposite leaves, which are typical of the mint family. However, the flowers of field mint have petals that are similar in size and shape, unlike the 2-lipped flowers of most other plants in the mint family. The small blue, purple, or pink flowers of field mint form in clusters that are located in the leaf axils.

July–September.

Habitat/Range: Stream banks, lakeshores, and ditches from the lowlands to the subalpine forest.

Comments: Hikers and canoeists often smell the strong mint aroma of field mint, crushed underfoot, before they see it. The herb is gathered for its flavor and medicinal value.

Siberian Chives

SIBERIAN CHIVES
Allium schoenoprasum L.
Lily Family (Liliaceae)

Description: Chives are perennial herbs growing from clusters of bulbs. The flowers have 3 lilac-colored petals and sepals, which are alike in size and shape. The flowers are arranged in an umbel at the top of the plant, with all the flower pedicels attached at a common point, as an umbrella. The flowers begin blooming from the center of the arrangement and progress outward to the perimeter. The leaves are round and hollow, and all parts of the plant have a strong onion aroma and flavor.

April–August.

Habitat/Range: Wet meadows and along stream banks and lakeshores.

Comments: Plants in the genus *Allium* (including chives, onions, and garlic) have long been cultivated and used for food and flavoring. Wild Siberian chives is the same species that has been cultivated as chives for centuries.

BLUE CAMAS
Camassia quamash (Pursh) Greene
Lily Family (Liliaceae)

Description: Blue camas flowers are arranged in a raceme with a narrow, leafy bract below each flower. The sepals and petals vary in color from deep purple to pale blue and occasionally white. Each flower has 6 stamens and a single style, which often falls away as the capsule matures. Leaves are linear and arise from the base of the plant. A bulb (onionlike, but odorless) is the underground food storage organ for these perennial, herbaceous plants.

April–early July.

Habitat/Range: Moist mountain meadows.

Comments: *Camassia* and *quamash* are derived from the words applied to this plant by the Nimi'-pu, or Nez Perce, people. On September 20, 1805, William Clark, with an advance party of the Lewis and Clark Expedition, found Nez Perce people busily digging and preparing the blue camas for food at what is now Weippe Prairie, Idaho.

Blue Camas

CHOCOLATE LILY
Fritillaria atropurpurea Nutt.
Lily Family (Liliaceae)

Description: Chocolate lily has 1–4 flowers that hang downward like a bell. The 6 tepals (petals and petal-like sepals) are dark maroon to chocolate brown, with greenish white to yellow spots or mottles. There is a nectar-bearing gland at the base of each tepal. The linear leaves are distributed up the flowering stem. The plants are perennial from a cluster of small, underground bulblets.

April–July.

Habitat/Range: Open, grassy slopes in the foothills and in openings in the forest through the montane and lower subalpine zones.

Comments: *Fritillaria* comes from the Latin word *fritillus,* meaning "dice box," which refers to the squarish, dicelike capsule of these plants. Leopard lily, checker lily, and rice-root are other common names that have been applied to this plant.

Chocolate Lily

DOUGLAS' WILD HYACINTH
Triteleia grandiflora Lindl.
(Also *Brodiaea douglasii* Wats.)
Lily Family (Liliaceae)

Description: The blue flowers of wild hyacinth are arranged in an umbel on the end of a long stalk. The petals of wild hyacinth are joined together in a basal tube for about half their length. The leaves of wild hyacinth are basal, with no leaves on the 8–28" long flower stalk. The plants store food in solid, bulblike underground stems called corms.

May–July.

Habitat/Range: Well-drained soils of grasslands, sagebrush steppes, and woodlands in the valleys and foothills to moderate elevations in the mountains.

Comments: *Triteleia* comes from the Greek words *trios* (three) and *teleios* (complete). This plant was first discovered and described by Meriwether Lewis on April 17, 1806, near present-day The Dalles, Oregon. Lewis wrote in his journal on that date: "there is a species of hiasinth in these plains the bulb of which the natives eat either boiled baked or dried in the sun. this bulb is white, not entirely solid, and of a flat form; the bulb of the present year overlays, or crowns that of the last and seems to be pressed close to it. . . . this hiasinth is of a pale blue colour and is a very pretty flower."

Douglas' Wild Hyacinth

BLUE FLAX
Linum lewisii Pursh
Flax Family (Linaceae)

Description: In early summer, the bright blue flowers of blue flax wave above the grasses as if suspended there. Each flower has 5 sepals,

Blue Flax

5 petals, 5 stamens, and 5 styles. The styles are considerably longer than the stamens. The leaves are narrow and alternate on the slender stems. The plants are perennial from a woody base and taproot.

May–July.

Habitat/Range: Well-drained and dry soils of the prairie grasslands and in openings in the forest from the foothills all the way up to the alpine mountaintops.

Comments: *Linum lewisii* was named in honor of Meriwether Lewis by Frederick Pursh in 1814, in his manual *Flora Americae Septentrionalis.* Pursh described the species in this book from a plant collected by Lewis on July 9, 1806, along the Sun River in Montana. The seeds of blue flax were used as food by Native Americans of the Missouri River, both for their flavor and nutritive value. The plants were also used medicinally by Shoshone people to treat sore eyes and as a poultice to reduce swellings. The strong fibers of the stems were twisted into fishing line and other cordage.

STRIPED CORALROOT
Corallorhiza striata Lindl.
Orchid Family (Orchidaceae)

Description: Coralroot orchids have no green leaves in which to conduct photosynthesis. They obtain their nutrients and energy from parasitizing fungi, which in turn obtain these substances from live plants or rotting organic matter on the forest floor. The leaves are reduced to tubular sheaths that enclose and conceal the purple stem below. Flowers are borne in an unbranched raceme along the upper half of the stem. The sepals and petals are yellowish pink with prominent reddish brown to purple stripes.

June–July.

Habitat/Range: Aspen, coniferous forests.

Comments: Coralroots are so named for their many branched underground stems, or rhizomes, that look superficially like branches of sea coral. They have no true roots. The coralroots live in a symbiotic relationship with fungi in the humus layer of the forest floor. They may not send up a flowering stem for years, until conditions are favorable for successful reproduction.

Striped Coralroot

Giant Helleborine

GIANT HELLEBORINE
Epipactis gigantea Dougl.
Orchid Family (Orchidaceae)

Description: As the name implies, these are large plants, 1–3' tall or more. The numerous leaves clasp the stem. The lowest leaves are oval but quickly become lance-shaped up the stem. Several (3–9) flowers occur in a raceme arrangement along the upper part of the stem. The sepals are greenish yellow with purple veins. The petals are similar but are rose with purple veins. The hinged lip is the most colorful petal, having a pink, heart-shaped tip. These perennial, herbaceous plants reproduce vegetatively by strong underground stems.

April–early August.

Habitat/Range: Wet soil of seeps, springs, and streams; in the northern part of its range it grows best near hot springs. This orchid species is rare in the Central Rocky Mountains, listed as "sensitive" by the USDA Forest Service in MT, WY, and ID.

Comments: Chatterbox is another common name for this plant. The rapid movement of the hinged lip, with the slightest breeze, resembles the lower jaw of a funny little elf, gabbing away.

Brown's Peony

BROWN'S PEONY
Paeonia brownii Dougl.
Peony Family (Paeoniaceae)

Description: The peony family is closely related to the buttercup family (Ranunculaceae). Peonies have numerous spirally arranged stamens and several superior pistils, like most plants in the buttercup family. However, peonies are unique in having leathery persistent sepals, pistils enclosed by a disk, and many stamens that develop from the center outward toward the perimeter. Brown's peony is the only species in the peony family that is native to the Central Rocky Mountains. The large, brownish purple to red flowers and the deeply parted, bluish green leaves are distinctive; this peony is not likely to be confused with any other plant in this area.

May–June.

Habitat/Range: Sagebrush steppes and dry forests from the foothills to the montane forest zone; southwestern half of the Central Rocky Mountains from southeastern WA, eastern OR, and south-central ID to Teton County, WY.

Comments: The name *Paeonia* comes from the ancient Greek *Paeon,* the physician of the gods, who used the plant medicinally according to legend. Shoshone and other Native American peoples used a decoction of the roots of Brown's peony internally to treat tuberculosis, venereal disease, coughs, nausea, diarrhea, and kidney trouble. The root was also used externally to treat headache, swellings, boils, and wounds. Herbalists have used peony for a variety of conditions including melancholia, painful or excessive menstruation, uterine cramping, prostatitis, spasmodic coughing, muscle pain, and stress.

SHOWY JACOB'S LADDER
Polemonium pulcherrimum Hook.
Phlox Family (Polemoniaceae)

Description: Jacob's ladder differs from other members of the phlox family by having an herbaceous, green calyx tube of uniform texture and color. The compound leaves have many definite leaflets arranged pinnately along the main axis. Showy jacob's ladder has a petal tube that is about as wide as it is long. The plants are usually less than 1' tall, although the variety *calycinum* is often taller (up to 20" high). The plants are covered with glandular hairs.

May–August.

Habitat/Range: Montane, subalpine, alpine.

Comments: *Polemonium* is said to have been named either for the Greek philosopher, Polemon, or for the Greek word *polemos,* meaning "strife." The glandular hairs of showy jacob's ladder impart a mildly foul odor to some plants, while others are essentially odorless.

Showy Jacob's Ladder

Pygmy Bitterroot

PYGMY BITTERROOT
Lewisia pygmaea (Gray) Robins
Purslane Family (Portulacaceae)

Description: The small flowers of pygmy bitterroot vary in color from white to pink or purple. There are 2 small, opposite, leaflike bracts about midway up the flowering stem. Each stem has a single flower. The flowers have 2 oval sepals with tiny teeth on the margin, and about 7 petals. The leaves all originate from the plant base and are narrow and up to 6" long. The flowering stems are much shorter than the leaves.

May–August.

Habitat/Range: Subalpine, alpine.

Comments: The German botanist Frederick Pursh named the genus *Lewisia* in honor of Meriwether Lewis (1774–1809) of the Lewis and Clark Expedition.

MOUNTAIN DOUGLASIA
Douglasia montana Gray
Primrose Family (Primulaceae)

Description: Mountain douglasia is a ground-hugging cushion plant. The small linear to lance-shaped leaves form basal rosettes, tightly grouped to form mats. The flowering stems are leafless, each with a single, showy flower. The sepals are tubular with 5 keeled and pointed lobes. The pink to violet flower is wheel-shaped, with a short petal tube and wide, horizontally flaring limbs.

*Late March–early April (foothills);
June–early July (alpine).*

Habitat/Range: Foothills, alpine.

Comments: *Douglasia* was named in honor of David Douglas (1798–1834), an early plant collector in the northwestern United States. The pink-flowered cushions of *Douglasia* are sometimes mistaken for a common companion, moss campion (*Silene acaulis*). However, *Douglasia* petals are fused together to form a tube at the base, while moss campion petals only appear tubular. When the tubular calyx of moss campion is removed, the individual, separate petals can be seen. Also, the stamens and style of *Douglasia* are hidden within the petal tube, while the stamens and style of moss campion protrude far beyond the flaring petals.

Mountain Douglasia

MONKSHOOD
Aconitum columbianum Nutt.
Buttercup Family (Ranunculaceae)

Description: Monkshood looks a lot like larkspur, but the upper sepal forms a hood that conceals the 2 true petals. The sepals are petal-like and brightly colored from blue to deep purple, or occasionally white or cream colored. Plants are 1–7' tall or taller, with numerous leaves up the flowering stem that are deeply cleft and toothed.

June–August.

Habitat/Range: Subalpine.

Comments: *Aconitum* comes from the Greek *akoniton* (leopard poison), or possibly from the name Aconis, an ancient city of Bithynia in Asia Minor. *Aconitum* species contain poisonous diterpene alkaloids (aconitine) that range widely in their toxicity. Some are deadly poisonous. Our western mountain monkshood is probably not one of the extremely deadly species, but it has been blamed for some livestock losses. The main symptoms of poisoning are numbness and paralysis of the extremities and respiratory system. In ancient times a decoction of aconite was given

Monkshood

to criminals as fatal punishment. Trained herbalists have used the plant topically for pain and internally for acute inflammation, but this should not be tried by the amateur.

PASQUEFLOWER
Anemone patens L.
(Also *Pulsatilla hirsutissima* (Pursh) Brit.)
Buttercup Family (Ranunculaceae)

Description: Pasqueflower has basal leaves and 3 leafy bracts on the flowering stem, topped by a single, large, purple flower. The flower has many stamens and pistils. Each pistil has a style that persists as a long plumelike beak on the capsule. The leaves have 2–4" long stalks. The blades of the leaves are deeply cut into many long, narrow segments. The entire plant is covered by long, silky, straight hairs. It is often confused with sugar bowl (*Clematis hirsutissima*), which it resembles. However, sugar bowl has numerous opposite leaves on the flowering stem and no basal leaves. Pasqueflowers are among the first flowers to announce the coming of spring, with flowers sometimes pushing through the snow to bloom in late March.

March–August.

Pasqueflower

Habitat/Range: Foothills to alpine.

Comments: *Anemone* is from the Greek word *anemos*, "the wind," which employed flowers to herald its coming. Strong winds are common in pasqueflower habitat and the flowers are sometimes called windflower. It is the floral emblem of South Dakota and Manitoba.

SHORT-STYLED COLUMBINE
Aquilegia brevistyla Hook.
Buttercup Family (Ranunculaceae)

Short-Styled Columbine

Description: The blue, fishhook-shaped spurs and yellow petal blades distinguish short-styled columbine from other columbines in the Central Rocky Mountains. The flowers are smaller (less than ¾" long) than other species in the area and are covered with fine hair. The plants are 8–32" tall. The basal leaves are much shorter than the stems. The style, or beak of the capsule, is very short (³/₁₆" or less).

Late June–July.

Habitat/Range: Open woods, meadow margins, and along streams in the lower subalpine and upper montane forests; Judith River basin of the Little Belt Mountains of MT.

Comments: *Aquilegia* may have originated from the Latin *aquila,* or "eagle." With a little imagination the spurs of columbine flowers do resemble eagle claws, especially the curved or hooked spurs of species like short-styled columbine. Short-styled columbine is rare in the Central Rocky Mountains and is listed as a sensitive plant species in the Lewis and Clark National Forest.

Limestone Columbine

LIMESTONE COLUMBINE

Aquilegia jonesii Parry
Buttercup Family (Ranunculaceae)

Description: The large, purple flowers of lime-stone columbine seem out of proportion to the small plants they grow on and are truly worth looking for. They are low, ground-hugging plants with leafless stems, seldom more than 4" tall, that bear a single flower (or sometimes 2). The leaves are all basal and densely crowded together near the ground surface. The flowers are quite showy, blue to purple with short (½" long), straight spurs. It sometimes hybridizes with yellow columbine (*A. flavescens*), produc-ing a tall plant having large flowers with straight purple spurs and petals but yellow sepal blades.

June–July.

Habitat/Range: Calcareous soils on alpine and subalpine ridgetops and upper slopes. It has a narrow geographic range along the Rocky Mountain Continental Divide, and island ranges from southern Alberta through MT to northern WY.

Comments: Most of the wildflowers found in the Central Rocky Mountains also occur in the adjacent mountain and/or plains regions of North America in one direction or another. Some are even found across the seas in Europe and Asia as well. However, limestone colum-bine makes its home only here in the high mountains of the Central and Northern Rockies; it is one of our few regional endemics, found nowhere else in the world.

Western Virgin's Bower

WESTERN VIRGIN'S BOWER
Clematis occidentalis (Hornem.) DC.
(Also *C. columbiana* (Nutt.) T. & G.,
misapplied)
Buttercup Family (Ranunculaceae)

Description: Western virgin's bower is a vine
having compound leaves with only 3 leaflets.
The similar Columbia virgin's bower (*C.
columbiana*) has 6 or 9 leaflets per compound
leaf. Flowers are purple or blue, and large and
showy. The stem of the leaf often winds around
tree branches or other plants as it climbs up,
searching for light under the shade of the forest
canopy.

May–July.

Habitat/Range: Shady forests, on cliffs, and in
thickets of the montane and subalpine zones.

Comments: *Clematis* is from the Greek word
clema, a "plant shoot or vine." *Clematis* species
are relatives of buttercups (genus *Ranunculus*),
and it is suspected that they may contain similar toxic properties. Shoshone and other Native
Americans used virgin's bower externally as a
poultice to reduce swellings or to bring boils to
a head and for rheumatic pain. Trained herbalists have used the plant as a liniment and for
migraine headaches, but the amateur should not
try this because of the toxic properties.

TALL MOUNTAIN LARKSPUR
Delphinium glaucum Wats.
Buttercup Family (Ranunculaceae)

Tall Mountain Larkspur

Description: Tall mountain larkspur is often 5' tall or more. The upper sepal of larkspur has a long projection, or spur, on the back, but there is no hood as there is in monkshood. The sepals are showy, like petals, and project forward. The large, showy flowers are bluish purple to lavender, and usually number 25 or more per stem. Below the flowers the stems are without hairs but are covered with a fine, white, powdery substance that readily rubs off.

July–August.

Habitat/Range: Cool, wet meadows, bogs, along stream sides, and in open, coniferous woods of the subalpine forest.

Comments: *Delphinium* is derived from the Greek word *delphin,* or "dolphin," perhaps from a resemblance of the flower to the sea mammal. It is called "larkspur" because it looks like the spur on the foot of the lark. Larkspurs are poisonous plants that have caused sickness and death in domestic livestock. Tall larkspur poisoning is responsible for more cattle losses than any other poisonous plant in the Rocky Mountains. It is most toxic during its youngest growth stage, when the alkaloids are most concentrated. Trained herbalists have used a tincture of larkspur seed externally to kill body lice.

WYOMING KITTENTAILS
Besseya wyomingensis (A. Nels.) Rydb.
Figwort Family (Scrophulariaceae)

Description: The violet to purple color of these flowers comes from the brightly colored filaments of the stamens. Each small flower has 2 hairy sepals and 2 stamens, but no petals. The flowers are densely crowded in a spikelike arrangement on the end of the simple stem. The largest leaves have long petioles that come from the base of the plant. The leaves on the flowering stem are without petioles and get progressively smaller up the stem. The margin of the leaves have fine teeth.

April–July.

Habitat/Range: Grasslands from the plains to the high mountains.

Comments: *Besseya* was named in honor of Charles E. Bessey (1845–1915), a professor of

Wyoming Kittentails

botany at the University of Nebraska. It is among the first wildflowers to bloom in the Central Rockies.

Showy Indian Paintbrush

SHOWY INDIAN PAINTBRUSH
Castilleja pulchella Rydb.
Figwort Family (Scrophulariaceae)

Description: Showy Indian paintbrush is a low-growing (less than 6" tall) wildflower of the alpine summits. The most colorful parts of Indian paintbrush flowers are usually the leafy bracts and sepals, rather than the petals. The bracts of showy Indian paintbrush vary in color from deep purple to occasionally yellow. The sepals are also mostly purple, though sometimes they are purple tipped and yellow toward the base. The petal tube is rather inconspicuous, barely extending beyond the sepals. The upper petal segment (galea) is short, much less than half the length of the entire petal tube. Like the bracts and sepals, the margin of the petal tube is purple, becoming yellow below. The upper leaves and bracts have a pair of short, lateral lobes. The lower leaves are entire. The entire plant is covered with soft, glandular hair.

June–August.

Habitat/Range: Alpine, subalpine; southwestern MT, western WY.

Comments: *Castilleja* is named for the Spanish botanist, Domingo Castillejo. *Pulchella* means "beautiful," a good name for these lovely wildflowers. The various species of *Castilleja* are among the most difficult to distinguish; many of the distinguishing features intergrade from one species to another.

Splitleaf Indian Paintbrush

SPLITLEAF INDIAN PAINTBRUSH
Castilleja rhexifolia Rydb.
Figwort Family (Scrophulariaceae)

Description: This Indian paintbrush of the subalpine meadows is intermediate in height (mostly 6–12" tall). The bracts and sepals are a brilliant rose-purple or magenta. The upper petal segment (galea) is shorter than the petal tube but much longer than the short, green lower lip. The petal tube extends well beyond the sepals. The leaves are lance-shaped and usually entire (not lobed). The bracts, below each flower, normally have a pair of short lateral lobes. This species is most often confused with scarlet Indian paintbrush (*Castilleja miniata* Dougl.), which is a taller plant (mostly greater than 12" tall), with deeply cut bracts and scarlet flowers.

June–August.

Habitat/Range: Meadows of the subalpine and alpine.

Comments: *Rhexifolia* means "splitleaf," probably in reference to the lobed leafy bracts or to the occasional lobed leaf. It seems like an inappropriate name, since the leaves are normally entire, or uncut. The species was named from a specimen collected by two prominent botanists, Per Axel Rydberg and Ernst Bessey, on Cedar Mountain in Madison County, Montana, on July 16, 1897. At the time, Rydberg and Bessey were collecting plant specimens on the first official botanical field trip for the New York Botanical Garden. This is the most common high-mountain Indian paintbrush of the Central Rocky Mountains. It seems to gather the bright alpine sunlight and glow, as if from its own inner fire.

Lewis' Monkey-Flower

LEWIS' MONKEY-FLOWER
Mimulus lewisii Pursh
Figwort Family (Scrophulariaceae)

Description: The bright magenta to pink flowers of Lewis' monkey-flower are brilliant along the streams of the Central Rocky Mountains. Each flower has 2 lips: the upper lip is 2-lobed and the lower lip is 3-lobed. The lower lip is marked with 2 yellow, hairy ridges. The flower stalks (pedicels) originate in the leaf axils and are much longer than the tubular sepals. The sepals have 5 keeled ribs, terminating in sharp teeth about equal in size. These ribs are often reddish tinged. The leaves form pairs attached directly to the main branch. There are coarse teeth on the margin of the leaves. The plants are perennial from underground stems, and quite tall (1–3½').

July–August.

Habitat/Range: Stream sides in the subalpine and alpine zones.

Comments: *Mimulus* is from the Latin word for a "comic," in reference to the "smiling face" appearance of the flower. This plant was named *Lewisii* in honor of Meriwether Lewis of the Lewis and Clark Expedition. Frederick Pursh described and illustrated this species for the first time in *Flora Americae Septentrionalis* in 1814. He credited his knowledge of this plant to a specimen that Lewis collected in August 1805, "on the headsprings of the Missouri, at the foot of Portage Hill," which was probably near Lemhi Pass, in Beaverhead County, Montana. Unfortunately, this specimen has been lost to science.

Fernleaf Lousewort

FERNLEAF LOUSEWORT
Pedicularis cystopteridifolia Rydb.
Figwort Family (Scrophulariaceae)

Description: Fernleaf lousewort has purple, tubular flowers. The upper lip petal (galea) arches above the 3-lobed lower lip. The leaves are pinnately compound with segments arranged opposite each other along the central leaf axis. The individual leaf segments are again deeply cut or cleft. The leaflike bracts below each flower are quite different from the leaves. Beyond the basal portion the bracts are long, narrow, and not cut or segmented. The plants are 4–18" tall. It is most likely to be confused with Parry's lousewort (see p. 57).

June–August.

Habitat/Range: Open meadows and on grassy slopes from moderate to high elevations in the mountains from the subalpine to the alpine zones. It is endemic to the Central Rocky Mountains, found in this region from northern and western WY to southwestern MT, and nowhere else in the world.

Comments: *Pedicularis* is from a Latin word meaning "louse," originating from a superstition that livestock grazing on these plants were more apt to have lice. Louseworts are partially parasitic, attaching themselves to the roots of host plants and deriving a portion of their nutrition from them. They are difficult to grow in the garden, possibly because of the lack of a suitable host species, and are best left to beautify their native landscape.

Parry's Lousewort

PARRY'S LOUSEWORT
Pedicularis parryi A. Gray
Figwort Family (Scrophulariaceae)

Description: Parry's lousewort has purple flowers and pinnately compound leaves, much like fernleaf lousewort (see above). It differs from fernleaf lousewort by having an upper flower petal with a short, straight beak and floral bracts with segments much like the leaves. The ultimate leaf segments of Parry's lousewort are merely toothed and not again deeply cut, like fernleaf lousewort. The basal leaves of Parry's lousewort are more abundant than the sparse stem leaves.

July–August.

Habitat/Range: Moist meadows and on open slopes from the subalpine zone to the alpine.

Comments: *Pedicularis* is a very large genus and one of the most diverse in floral form. The elaborate flowers of the species in the Rockies are adapted for pollination by bees. In other parts of the world they have floral mechanisms specialized for pollination by various other insects or hummingbirds. Herbalists value *Pedicularis* species as a sedative tea to relax the muscles and quiet the nerves.

Taper-Leaved Beardtongue

TAPER-LEAVED BEARDTONGUE
Penstemon attenuatus Dougl.
Figwort Family (Scrophulariaceae)

Description: The clustered flowers of taper-leaved beardtongue vary in color from blue-purple (illustrated) to pink, yellow, or white. There are 5 stamens: 4 fertile ones bearing pollen, plus a sterile one. The anthers of the fertile stamens are smooth (hairless) and split open full length upon maturity. The end of the sterile stamen is covered with yellow hair that can be seen just inside the mouth of the petal tube. The outer surface of the petal tube, sepals, and upper stem are covered with glandular hairs. The leaves are attached opposite each other on the main stem, characteristic of all beardtongues (*Penstemon* species). The upper leaves are without a petiole (stem of the leaf), while the lower ones have a short petiole. The leaves are lance-shaped and mostly smooth on the margin. The common small-flowered beardtongue (*P. procerus*) is similar, but lacks the glandular hairs of taper-leaved beardtongue.

June–August.

Habitat/Range: Open, dry meadows, sagebrush steppes, and woods from the foothills to the subalpine zone; from eastern WA and southeastern OR west through ID to western MT and northwestern WY.

Comments: The genus name *Penstemon* is from the Latin word *paene,* meaning "almost," and the Greek word *stemon,* or "thread." This is in reference to the sterile staminode, which is almost (but not quite) a complete stamen. The origin of the word has also been attributed to the Greek word *pente,* meaning "five," in reference to the five stamens of *Penstemon.*

Rockvine Beardtongue

ROCKVINE BEARDTONGUE
Penstemon ellipticus Coult. & Fish.
Figwort Family (Scrophulariaceae)

Description: The flowers of rockvine beard-tongue are deep lavender and seem large and out of proportion to the low-growing plant. The 4 fertile anthers are covered with long, tangled, woolly hair that is visible to the naked eye. The sterile stamen is short and does not extend beyond the lips of the petal. The sepals and upper stems are covered with glandular hairs. The leaves are oval, rounded on the end, and attached with a short petiole. There are fine teeth along the margin of the leaves. The stems are often woody at the base and lie horizontally on the ground, where they root, forming large, dense mats.

Late June–September.

Habitat/Range: Rocky crevices, talus, and cliffs in the high mountains, often in the alpine zone; MT, central ID.

Comments: The name *ellipticus* refers to the leaves, which are shaped like an ellipse—egg-shaped or oblong with rounded ends.

CRESTED BEARDTONGUE
Penstemon eriantherus Pursh
Figwort Family (Scrophulariaceae)

Crested Beardtongue

Description: Crested beardtongue has purple flowers that vary from pale lavender to blue or deep violet. The lower petal lobes have long, yellow hair and dark "guidelines" that direct insects into the petal tube for pollination. The 4 fertile stamens have smooth (hairless) anthers that split open full length to distribute the pollen. The sterile stamen is covered with dense, yellow hair and is clearly visible sticking out of the petal tube. The entire plant is covered with hair and is glandular at least on the sepals and upper stems. It is an erect, herbaceous plant with leaves that can be either toothed or smooth on the margin.

May–July.

Habitat/Range: Dry plains, sagebrush slopes, and into the foothills and lower mountains.

Comments: *Eriantherus* means "woolly anthered." This is the classic "beardtongue." The sterile staminode is covered with golden hair and protrudes from the flower tube with the appearance of a bearded tongue sticking out of the mouth of some bizarre animal.

SHINING BEARDTONGUE
Penstemon nitidus Dougl. ex Benth.
Figwort Family (Scrophulariaceae)

Description: The bright blue flowers of shining beardtongue present a sharp contrast to the harsh habitat in which they often grow. The 4 fertile stamens have smooth (hairless) anthers that split open full length. The sterile stamen is covered with long, bright yellow hair that is visible in the mouth of the flower. The plants are herbaceous, 4–12" tall. The leaves are broadly lance-shaped. The stems and leaves are smooth and covered with a whitish substance that rubs off (called a glaucous coating).

May–July.

Habitat/Range: Grasslands, foothills, and the talus slopes in the mountains of the eastern portion of the Central Rockies in MT and WY.

Comments: *Nitidus* mean "shiny" or "glossy," and this plant does look as if it has been polished. The glaucous foliage reflects the sun's rays, giving the plants a shiny appearance.

Shining Beardtongue

Payette Beardtongue

PAYETTE BEARDTONGUE
Penstemon payettensis Nels. & Macbr.
Figwort Family (Scrophulariaceae)

Description: The bright blue flowers of Payette beardtongue are often tinged with purple. The flowers are rather large (¾–1⅛"). The 4 fertile anther sacs are straight and smooth, except for minute hairs or teeth on the sutures where they split open. The sterile stamen varies from hairless to sparsely hairy and is rather inconspicuous. The leaves and stems are smooth (hairless), glossy, and deep green. There are several other species of beardtongue with large, bright blue flowers and smooth leaves that could be mistaken for Payette beardtongue, especially dark blue beardtongue (*P. cyaneus*). However, these similar species have fertile anther sacs that are hairy and/or twisted. Observing these tiny differences requires a hand lens and a lot of patience.

May–August.

Habitat/Range: Openings in the forest on sandy or gravelly soils of the valleys and foothills up to moderate elevations in the mountains; southwestern portion of the Central Rocky Mountains from the Wallowa Mountains of OR to central ID between the Salmon River and the Snake River plains. It is also reported from Ravalli County, MT.

Comments: This flower was named *payettensis* in honor of the Payette River and the Payette National Forest in Idaho where it was first discovered.

Cusick's Speedwell

CUSICK'S SPEEDWELL

Veronica cusickii Gray
Figwort Family (Scrophulariaceae)

Description: The violet-blue flowers of Cusick's speedwell have 4 sepals, 4 petals, 2 stamens, and a single style. The flowers are wheel-shaped: circular and flat, about ⅜–½" wide. The petals are irregular, with the upper one broad and the lower one the narrowest. The filaments are about ¼" long and very conspicuous. The style is even longer (⅜"). The stems are simple, about 6" tall, and terminated by the flower arrangement. Glandular hairs cover the surface of the stems, especially within the flower arrangement. The leaves are egg-shaped, smooth, and are arranged in pairs opposite each other on the stem.

July–early September.

Habitat/Range: Moist, rocky slopes, in meadows, and along stream banks at high elevations in the subalpine and alpine zones: ID, western MT, OR, WA.

Comments: The origin of the name *Veronica* is unknown, but it may honor St. Veronica, who is said to have offered a cloth to Christ upon which he wiped his face on his way to the crucifixion. Christ's face is said to have left an impression or "portrait" on the cloth. Such an impression is called a "veronica." *Cusickii* honors William A. Cusick, who first collected the plant in the alpine region of the Blue Mountains of Oregon.

Climbing Nightshade

CLIMBING NIGHTSHADE
Solanum dulcamara L.
Potato Family (Solanaceae)

Description: Climbing nightshade is an introduced vine, with blue to violet flowers and bright red berries. The petal lobes are much longer than the short tube, and turn back toward the stem as they mature. The flower arrangement is branched and includes 10–25 flowers. The leaves are egg-shaped to heart-shaped and sometimes have a pair of lobes at the base. The plants scramble over shrubs and other vegetation for support.

May–September.

Habitat/Range: Introduced; moist soil, often along rivers and streams, in thickets, open woods, and clearings.

Comments: *Solanum* is one of the larger genera worldwide, but it is concentrated in tropical and subtropical America. It includes the common potato (*Solanum tuberosum*). Many species of *Solanum* contain poisonous alkaloids, and grazing of climbing nightshade foliage has been responsible for causing livestock deaths. Another common name applied to this plant is bittersweet, and this name has led to confusion with an unrelated and edible species that is also called bittersweet (*Celastrus scandens*). The bright red berries of climbing nightshade are very attractive and tempting but should not be eaten.

BRACTED VERBENA
Verbena bracteata Lag. & Rodr.
Verbena Family (Verbenaceae)

Description: Verbenas resemble mints with their opposite leaves, squarish stems, and tubular flowers with 5 petal limb segments: 2 upper and 3 lower. However, verbenas are not aromatic like mints, and they lack the deeply 4-lobed ovary attached to the base of the style. Bracted verbena crawls or spreads along the surface on hairy horizontal stems 4–24" long. The leaves are toothed and have deeply cleft lower segments. The flowers are inconspicuous and almost hidden by the bracts. The petals vary in color from blue to pink or sometimes white.

May–September.

Habitat/Range: Disturbed soil anywhere from the cracks in city sidewalks to road cuts and barren slopes in the mountains.

Comments: *Verbena* is a Latin name for sacred boughs used in religious rites. Several species of *Verbena* have been used medicinally by Native American people and modern herbalists. Blue vervain (*Verbena hastata*) was used by the Teton Dakota people to make a drink as a remedy for stomachaches. Other tribes used the plant to treat fits and to clear up cloudy urine or stop

Bracted Verbena

nosebleeds. Herbalists have long used *Verbena* species to promote vomiting when needed. It also has value as a sedative and is used to reduce phlegm and to increase sweating and urination. It is especially useful in relieving the symptoms of the common cold.

Early Blue Violet

EARLY BLUE VIOLET
Viola adunca Sm.
Violet Family (Violaceae)

Description: The leaves of early blue violet are entire, egg-shaped to heart-shaped, and have finely rounded teeth on the margin. The leaves appear all basal in the early season, but leafy stems develop later that are up to 4" tall. The lowest petal has a conspicuous hooked spur over half its length. The lateral petals and the style are white bearded.

April–August.

Habitat/Range: Valleys to near timberline.

Comments: *Viola* is from the Latin *violaceous*, for the purple color (nearer blue). The common garden pansy is a species of *Viola*. Violets are edible fresh as a salad green or cooked.

PINK FLOWERS

Jeffrey's Shooting Star

Pink flowers grade into lavender on the blue end of the spectrum and red on the other end. Many species with pink flowers also have white flower variations. You may need to check the blue/purple, red, or white sections of this book if the flower you are searching for is not found here.

Dogbane

DOGBANE
Apocynum androsaemifolium L.
Dogbane Family (Apocynaceae)

Description: A dogbane flower has a pink, bell-shaped petal tube with 5 pointed lobes. The petal tube is more than twice the length of the sepals. The flowers are arranged on the end of the stem and sometimes in the upper leaf axils. The plants are herbaceous and 8–20" tall. The leaves are borne in pairs that droop downward from the stem, opposite each other. When broken, a white milky sap oozes from the leaves and stems. The long, narrow pods split open along a suture for seed distribution.

June–August.

Habitat/Range: Dry soil in the valleys and foothills, and the dry forests of the montane zone.

Comments: *Apocynum* is from two Greek words that mean "away from a dog." "Bane" means poison or death. Dogbane is a poisonous plant, but cases of poisoning are rare. Several chemical resins and glycosides have been isolated from the plant that are of medicinal value in the treatment of congestive heart failure; they increase the force of heart contractions. One of the side effects of ingesting the plant is nausea, and because of this the plant has been used to induce vomiting and is sometimes referred to as "wild ipecac." This is a dangerous plant, not for home use. Strong, supple fibers in the stems of this plant can be twisted into a fine cord for fishing line or other purposes.

Showy Mikweed

SHOWY MILKWEED
Asclepias speciosa Torr.
Milkweed Family (Asclepiadaceae)

Description: The pink flowers of showy milkweed are striking and very unusual. The 5 pink, lance-shaped petals are turned downward, concealing the 5 sepals. The 5 stamens are joined together and attached to the stigma. Each stamen has a large (½" long), lance-shaped hood that thrusts upward. Within the hood is a horn, attached to the base. The flowers are arranged in large clusters near the top of the plant. The leaves are 4–7" long and opposite on the stem. The plants are 2–4' tall and contain a milky latex.

May–August.

Habitat/Range: Disturbed soil of streams, ditches, cultivated fields, and roadsides.

Comments: *Asclepias* was named in honor of Aesculapius, the Greek physician and god of medicine. Various species of milkweed have a history of medicinal use in Europe and North America. Trained herbalists have used showy milkweed to stimulate expectoration, perspiration, and urination to increase expulsion of metabolic waste. The Shoshone Indians of Nevada used the latex of showy milkweed as an antiseptic and healing agent on sores. Other Native Americans used the ripe seed to draw out the poison of rattlesnake bites. The plant has been used for food, but it must be prepared properly to render it safe. This and several other species of milkweed have been found to contain various levels of poisonous resinoids, some causing livestock deaths. The "down" in the seedpods makes a fine insulating material.

Tweedy's Thistle

TWEEDY'S THISTLE
Cirsium tweedyi (Rydb.) Petr.
(Also *Cirsium polyphyllum* (Rydb.) Petr.)
Aster Family (Asteraceae)

Description: This native alpine thistle grows less than 3' tall and is very strongly spiny; more so than most thistles. The flower heads are stalkless (sessile), with several arranged along the upper stem or in a terminal cluster. The pink to white petal tube of an individual flower is short (less than ¾"). The leaves are narrow and deeply divided into pinnate segments (placed on either side of the axis, like a feather). Some plants have sparse, cobwebby hairs on the leaves, while others are smooth.

July–August.

Habitat/Range: Talus slopes and rocky alpine and subalpine ridges and summits. It is a regional endemic species occurring only in southwestern MT, northwestern WY, ID.

Comments: *Cirsium* comes from the Greek word *kirsos,* or "swollen vein." Thistles were supposed to be a remedy for swollen veins. Tweedy's thistle is named in honor of Frank Tweedy (1854–1937), a topographic engineer for the U.S. Geological Survey. Tweedy collected many new species of plants in his travels through Yellowstone National Park and the Pacific Northwest. Others named in his honor include Tweedy's rush and Tweedy's willow.

Wavy-Leaved Thistle

WAVY-LEAVED THISTLE
Cirsium undulatum (Nutt.) Spreng.
Aster Family (Asteraceae)

Description: Wavy-leaved thistle is 1–4' tall. There are several flower heads per plant, each one on the end of a long, leafy stem. The leafy bracts, around the base of each flower head, are dark green and shiny. Each bract has a lighter colored ridge down the back that is often glandular, or covered with a sticky substance. The pink to purple corolla of an individual flower is 1" or more in length. The stems and lower leaf surfaces are covered with densely matted, soft, white hair.

May–September.

Habitat/Range: Dry prairies and foothills and on open dry slopes in the valleys and low elevation mountains.

Comments: Wavy-leaved thistle is one of several native thistle species of the Central Rocky Mountains. The native thistles are a beautiful segment of our native flora, but they are often shunned because of their similarity to introduced thistles that are noxious weeds. Canada thistle (*C. arvense*), bull thistle (*C. vulgare*), and musk thistle (*Carduus nutans*) are pernicious alien species with pink to purple flowers that could be mistaken for wavy-leaved thistle or other native thistles. When attempting to control these noxious weed pests, one should be careful to make positive identification to avoid killing the numerous native thistle species that enrich our flora.

ROCKY MOUNTAIN BEE PLANT
Cleome serrulata Pursh
Caper Family (Capparidaceae)

Rocky Mountain Bee Plant

Description: This herbaceous annual reaches 1-3' tall or taller. The leaves are compound with 3 leaflets each. The pink (ranging from red to white) flowers are arranged in a terminal raceme that expands upward as the long flowering period progresses. Each flower has 4 sepals, 4 petals, and 6 stamens. The showy, pink filaments of the stamens project outward about twice the length of the petals. Flowers are borne on ¼-½" long (or longer) pedicels, which become the stalks of the single-celled capsules as the ovaries mature. The capsules arch downward from these long stalks.

June–August.

Habitat/Range: Disturbed or barren soil of the plains, foothills, and montane.

Comments: Rocky Mountain bee plant is well named. While it is in bloom, these plants are alive with several species of bees and flies seeking its nectar. Frederick Pursh named this plant from a specimen collected by Meriwether Lewis. Plains Indians used it for food, medicine, and in spiritual ceremonies.

TWINFLOWER
Linnaea borealis L.
Honeysuckle Family (Caprifoliaceae)

Description: Twinflower is a low-growing, evergreen, ground cover of the boreal forest. It spreads by horizontal stems on the surface of the organic layer of the forest floor. The small, egg-shaped leaves are in opposite pairs. Each leaf has a few shallow teeth on the margin of the upper half of the leaf. The leafy stems are short (less than 4" long) and bear a pair of pink flowers on the end of slender stalks. The bell-shaped flowers hang downward and are hairy on the inner surface.

June–September.

Habitat/Range: Cool, moist coniferous forests.

Twinflower

Comments: *Linnaea* was named for Carolus Linnaeus (1707–1778) and is said to have been his favorite flower. Linnaeus was professor of medicine and botany at Uppsala University in Sweden from 1742 until his death. In 1753, he wrote *Species Plantarum,* the basis for our present system of naming plant species.

MOSS CAMPION
Silene acaulis L.
Pink Family (Caryophyllaceae)

Description: Moss campion is a low, ground-hugging cushion plant. The dense cushions are up to a foot or more in diameter. The plants are usually about 2" tall but may be as much as 6". The bright, green leaves are narrow and arise from the base of the plant. The dead leaves from the previous seasons persist for years on the plants. The pink flowers are borne singly on short stalks up to 1½" long but are usually much shorter. The sepals are joined together into a tube that conceals the base of the entire petals. The 10 stamens and 3 styles extend well beyond the throat of the flower.

June–August.

Habitat/Range: Alpine fellfield, on windswept rocky ridges and summits above treeline.

Comments: Rock gardeners consider this one of the most beautiful and desirable rock garden plants.

Moss Campion

Hedge Bindweed

HEDGE BINDWEED
Calystegia sepium (L.) R. Br.
(Also *Convolvulus sepium* L.)
Morning-Glory Family (Convolvulaceae)

Description: Hedge bindweed has 1½–2½" large, pale pink to white funnel-shaped flowers. The flowers occur singly on the ends of 1½–5" long stalks from the leaf axils. A pair of broad, green, leafy bracts at the base of the flower conceals the sepals. The plant is a perennial vine up to 10' long and climbs over other plants for support. The leaves are heart-shaped with sharply angled lateral lobes.

July–August.

Habitat/Range: Introduced; moist soils along river bottoms and ditches in the valleys.

Comments: *Calystegia* comes from the Greek words *kalyx* (cup) and *stegos* (cover), in reference to the bracts that cover up the sepals (calyx). This beautiful wild morning-glory vine is also called lady's-nightcap, bell-bind, and Rutland beauty. It is closely related to field bindweed, a serious noxious weed.

KINNIKINNICK
Arctostaphylos uva-ursi (L.) Spreng.
Heath Family (Ericaceae)

Kinnikinnick

Description: Kinnikinnick is a forest ground cover. It has somewhat woody, horizontal stems that root and spread along the surface forming large mats. The leathery, evergreen leaves have a smooth margin (no teeth). The flowers are pink with petals that are fused into an urn shape, and hang downward like little Oriental lanterns. The red berries persist through winter.

April–June

Habitat/Range: Montane to alpine.

Comments: *Arctostaphylos* comes from the Greek word *arktos* (bear) and *staphyle* (bunch of grapes). *Uva* is Latin for "grape" and *ursi* is Latin for "bear." Both wild animals and humans eat the berries. *Uva-ursi* is an important medicinal herb for treating urinary tract infections and stones. "Kinnikinnick" is from a Native American word meaning "what you smoke." The tannin in the leaves has been used in tanning hides.

GROUSE HUCKLEBERRY
Vaccinium scoparium Leiberg
Heath Family (Ericaceae)

Description: Grouse huckleberry is a low shrub (less than 1' high) with numerous, broomlike stems. It often grows in large mats that cover the forest floor. The stems are green and strongly angled in cross section. The small (less than ⅝" long) leaves are lance-shaped, with fine teeth on the margin. The pink flower petals are joined together into an urn-shaped tube that hangs downward. The small (less than 3/16" in diameter) bright red berries are tart and very delicious.

May–August.

Habitat/Range: Cool, moist subalpine forests.

Comments: *Vaccinium* is the Latin name for blueberry. Other common names applied to plants in the genus include bilberry, cranberry, huckleberry, and whortleberry. Herbalists value *Vaccinium* species for their acidic, astringent properties. They use the herbs in treating diarrhea, ulcers, gum and skin inflammation, and urinary tract infections. Herbalists also use *Vaccinium* to assist in treating certain cases of diabetes and eye problems.

Grouse Huckleberry

SWAMP LAUREL

Kalmia microphylla (Hook.)
  Heller
(Also *Kalmia polifolia* Wang.)
Heath Family (Ericaceae)

Description: Swamp laurel is a low-growing (less than 6" tall) evergreen shrub. The leathery leaves are dark green above and gray-white beneath. The leaf margin is often rolled under but is sometimes flat. The pink flowers are large for the size of the plants and are very striking. The petals are fused together to form a shallow floral bowl. Within the flower "bowl" are 10 depressions that the stamens neatly fit within, while in bud. As the flower opens the stamens spring up from these depressions.

June–September.

Habitat/Range: Cool bogs, stream sides, and lakeshores in subalpine and alpine zones.

Swamp Laurel

Comments: *Kalmia* was named for Peter Kalm (1715–1779), a student of Carolus Linnaeus at Uppsala University in Sweden.

ALSIKE CLOVER

Trifolium hybridum L.
Bean Family (Fabaceae)

Description: Alsike clover is similar to the common white Dutch clover (*T. repens*), except the leafy stems of alsike clover rise upward and stand erect, instead of spreading over the ground and rooting at the nodes, as does white Dutch clover. Both species have typical 3-parted "clover" leaves, with leaflets that are egg-shaped to nearly round, and they have many flowers arranged in a tight head. As the flowers of alsike clover mature, they bend downward lending a hemispheric shape to the arrangement. The individual flowers are irregular, with banner, wing, and keel petals, as with all bean flowers. The pink to white flowers of alsike clover turn brownish with age.

May–September.

Habitat/Range: Introduced; disturbed places in the valleys, foothills, and montane zones.

Comments: Alsike is named for a place near Uppsala, Sweden, where it was observed by Carolus Linnaeus, the father of botanical nomenclature. Long-stalked clover (*T. longipes*), a widespread clover native to the United States, could be confused with alsike and white Dutch clover. However, long-stalked clover has longer and narrower leaves that are lance-shaped. The flowers of long-stalked clover are over ⅜" long, while alsike and white clover are less than ⅜" long. All clovers, native or introduced, are valuable forage plants and soil builders.

Alsike Clover

Fitweed Corydalis

FITWEED CORYDALIS

Corydalis caseana Gray
Fumitory Family (Fumariaceae)

Description: The unusual flowers of this plant have 4 pink petals in 2 pairs. The outer pair of petals are "hooded." The upper one has a narrow spur, about ½" long, that serves as a vessel for the nectar to attract pollinating insects. The inner pair of petals are joined together at their tip and enclose the stamen and pistil. There are many flowers (50–200) arranged in a simple or compound raceme on the end of the branches. The plants are perennial and quite tall, reaching 2–6' high or higher. The foliage has a gray-green appearance as a result of a glaucous coating—a fine, white powdery substance on the surface, which rubs off. The variety of this species that occurs in the Central Rocky Mountains is *cusickii,* which has a compact flower arrangement and a well-developed margin on the spurred upper petal.

June–August.

Habitat/Range: Beside streams; central ID, northeastern OR.

Comments: *Corydalis* comes from the Greek name for the "horned lark," probably because the spur of the flower resembles the spur on the head of the lark. The flowers are usually pollinated by bumblebees with long tongues that can reach to the nectar in the flower spur. The plants are rich in alkaloids that are toxic to sheep and cattle and have caused livestock deaths on the range. The name "fitweed" refers to the symptoms (convulsive spasms, bleating, and bawling) that livestock endure when poisoned by eating this plant.

Nettle-Leaved Horse-Mint

NETTLE-LEAVED HORSE-MINT

Agastache urticifolia (Benth.) Kuntze
Mint Family (Lamiaceae)

Description: Nettle-leaved horse-mint has the square stems, opposite leaves, and 2-lobed flowers typical of plants in the mint family. It is distinguished from its close relatives by a combination of the following characteristics: the style and stamens extend well beyond the petal tube; it has 4 stamens arranged in pairs, with one pair extending much further from the tube than the other pair; the plants are large and coarse, 1–5' tall; and the lower leaf surface is smooth or only sparsely covered with long hairs.

June–August.

Habitat/Range: Moist to rather dry slopes and in draws and open woods from the foothills to the lower subalpine zone.

Comments: *Agastache* comes from the Greek words *agan* (much) and *stachys* (ear of grain), in reference to the appearance of the dense flower arrangement. *Urticifolia* means that the foliage (*folia*) looks like that of nettle (*Urtica*), with its similar opposite, lanceolate, toothed leaves. Species of *Agastache* have been used by Native Americans for treating indigestion, chest pains related to coughing, and colds; inducing sweating; and cooling fevers. Modern herbalists have also relied on it to induce sweating and for the astringent, sedative properties it possesses. It has been used to treat headaches, urinary tract infections, sore throats, and minor wounds.

WILD BERGAMOT
Monarda fistulosa L.
Mint Family (Lamiaceae)

Description: The strong, pleasant, minty aroma is the first thing noticed about wild bergamot. This herbaceous plant is about 1–2' tall, and it has the square stems, opposite leaves, and 2-lipped flowers that characterize most mints. The narrow upper lip of the flower is long and arches over the lower, downturned lip. The 2 stamens and single style extend just beyond the upper lip.

June–September.

Habitat/Range: Moist openings and lightly shaded woods in the valleys, foothills, and montane forests.

Comments: The name *Monarda* honors Nicolas Monarda (1493–1588), a Spanish physician and botanist. This plant has also been called bee balm and Oswego tea, for a pleasant medicinal tea can be brewed from the leaves and flowers of wild bergamot. Native Americans used this herbal tea for stomachaches and externally for skin eruptions. It was also used as an aromatic hair rinse. It is reported to have been one of the plants used ceremonially in the Sun Dance. Herbalists use the plant to induce sweating and for its antiseptic and anesthetic properties. A leaf chewed and placed against the gum often deadens the pain of a sore tooth.

Wild Bergamot

MOUNTAIN HOLLYHOCK
Iliamna rivularis (Dougl.) Greene
Mallow Family (Malvaceae)

Description: Like all mallows, mountain hollyhock has flowers with many stamens that are joined together by their filaments to form a tube. The numerous anthers are free from the tube. The styles run through the tube, exiting above. Mountain hollyhock has large pink petals (greater than ¾" long) and 2–6" long leaves. The leaves are 3–7-lobed and toothed, resembling maple or grape leaves. The plants often grow 3–6' tall or more.

June–August.

Habitat/Range: Moist, disturbed forest openings from the foothills to the subalpine zones.

Comments: *Rivularis* is Latin for "brook-loving." Mountain hollyhock likes the moist soil near streams. It is particularly abundant after a forest fire.

Mountain Hollyhock

Short-Styled Onion

SHORT-STYLED ONION
Allium brevistylum Wats.
Lily Family (Liliaceae)

Description: The leaves of short-styled onion are flat and solid and arise from the base of the plant. The entire plant has a strong onion odor. The main flowering stem (scape) is also flat and solid with a narrow ridge along the upper margin. The ultimate stalks (pedicels) of the flowers come together at a common point, like an umbrella. The flower arrangement rises well above the tallest leaves. The pink petals are much longer than the very short style and stamen.

June–August.

Habitat/Range: Moist meadows, wooded slopes, and along stream sides from the moist montane and subalpine zones to the edge of the alpine; central MT, northeastern ID,WY.

Comments: The flowers of short-styled onion start blooming from the outer margin of the umbel and progress toward the center. In contrast, Siberian chives (*A. schoenoprasum*) blooms from the center outward. This and all *Allium* species have the distinctive odor and taste of onion or garlic and are good food plants. They have also been long valued for their antibacterial medicinal properties. The Cheyenne people used short-styled onion as a poultice to open carbuncles. Other Native American people used onions to treat coughs, vomiting, ear infections, colds, headaches, sinus problems, and bee stings.

Fireweed

FIREWEED
Epilobium angustifolium L.
Evening-Primrose Family (Onagraceae)

Description: Fireweed and willow herbs (*Epilobium* species) have seeds with a tuft of long hairs on the tip that carries the seeds aloft in the wind to new, faraway places to germinate. The sepals and petals are attached to the top of the long, narrow ovary, which itself resembles a stout flower stalk: the long style extends out beyond the stamens and ends in a prominent 4-cleft stigma. The leaves are narrow and 4–6" long, and the plants are 3–9' tall.

June–September.

Habitat/Range: Disturbed soils from the valleys to the subalpine zone.

Comments: *Epilobium* is derived from the Greek *epi* (upon) and *lobos* (pod), referring to the inferior ovary with the flower attached upon the top of the fruit. Like mountain hollyhock, fireweed is especially abundant on moist soils after a forest fire; hence the name. Because the seed is distributed readily by the wind, fireweed often spreads rapidly, becoming the dominant species for the first few years following a forest fire. The bright, pink flowers provide a brilliant contrast to the blackened trees and forest floor. It has a reputation as a nutritious, wild edible plant and as an astringent and anti-inflammatory herb. The herb is useful in treating diarrhea, hemorrhoids, and other conditions.

Butterfly-Weed

BUTTERFLY-WEED
Gaura coccinea (Nutt.) Pursh
Evening-Primrose Family (Onagraceae)

Description: Butterfly-weed is 8–24" tall with simple, shallowly toothed leaves, and in many ways resembles its close relatives, the willow herbs (*Epilobium* species). Both have flowers attached to the top of the ovary, with 4 sepals, 4 petals, and 8 stamens. However, the fruit of butterfly-weed is hard, nutlike, and does not split open like willow herbs. The style of a butterfly-weed flower extends beyond the stamens. The stigma is a dense, headlike cluster with 4 tiny lobes. The sepals bend sharply backward. Butterfly-weed flowers are pink, red, or nearly white.

June–August.

Habitat/Range: Dry, open slopes of grassland and sagebrush areas in the plains, valleys and foothills.

Comments: The name *Gaura* is derived from the Greek word *gauros* (superb; proud), probably because the flowers stand erect or "proud" on the end of the stems. Butterfly-weed has been used in herbal folk medicine to treat rheumatism, burns, inflammation, and pain. The Dakota people chewed and rubbed the plants on their hands before going to catch horses.

Fairy-Slipper

FAIRY-SLIPPER
Calypso bulbosa (L.) Oakes
Orchid Family (Orchidaceae)

Description: Fairy-slipper is most often confused with lady's slippers (*Cypripedium* species) and was initially placed in that genus by Linnaeus in 1753. Both have flowers with an inflated saclike lip petal. However, unlike lady's slippers, the lip of fairy-slipper has a flat apron with 3 short rows of white or yellow hairs on its surface, and 2 short spurs near the tip. Fairy-slipper has a single, egg-shaped basal leaf, while lady's slippers have 2 or more leaves, often on the flowering stem. Fairy-slipper has a single anther, while lady's slippers have 2.

May–July.

Habitat/Range: Cool, coniferous forests and bogs of the montane and subalpine forests. There are two varieties of fairy-slipper in North America. The variety *americana* (illustrated) has dense, yellow hair on the lip apron. It is most common in the Central Rocky Mountains and ranges from Alaska east through Canada and the Great Lakes states to Maine and Newfoundland and south in the Rocky Mountains to New Mexico and Arizona. The variety *occidentalis* has sparse white hair on the apron and is found from British Columbia south to California and east to northern Idaho.

Comments: *Calypso* is named for the legendary sea nymph of Homer's *Odyssey,* perhaps because of the secluded haunts of this orchid. Fairy-slipper and other orchids have very specialized reproduction systems, requiring exacting habitat conditions. With the human development of wild forests, so follows the decline of these sensitive wildflowers. We can help by protecting fairy-slipper habitat from disturbance and by not picking or collecting these precious gems of the forest.

Bitterroot

BITTERROOT
Lewisia rediviva Pursh
Purslane Family (Portulacaceae)

Description: When in full, glorious bloom the bitterroot is unmistakable. However, in its vegetative state it is inconspicuous; a basal rosette of small leaves (2" tall or less) growing close to the ground. The leaves first appear with the fall rains. They are narrow and succulent, almost round in cross section. The leaves resume growth in early spring, during flower bud development, but wither by the time the flowers are fully opened. The flowers are large and very beautiful. They have 5–9 sepals and 12–18 petals. Both sepals and petals are showy and vary in color from deep pink to rose or sometimes white.

May–July.

Habitat/Range: Dry, exposed slopes and poorly developed soils; in sagebrush in the valleys and foothills and up into the dry, open montane forests.

Comments: *Lewisia* was named in honor of Meriwether Lewis, who collected a specimen of bitterroot on July 1, 1806, near the present town of Lolo, Montana, during the Lewis and Clark Expedition. Lewis attached a note to the specimen, stating "The Indians eat the root of this Near Clark's R." "Clark's River" is now the Bitterroot River, named in honor of the plant. As noted by Lewis, the bitterroot was an important food plant of many Native American tribes. Legends associated with the bitterroot attest to the importance of this plant in their culture. Still important in our culture today, it is the floral emblem of Montana.

SCARLET GILIA
Ipomopsis aggregata (Pursh) Grant
(Also *Gilia aggregata* (Pursh) Spreng.)
Phlox Family (Polemoniaceae)

Description: Scarlet gilia is normally a biennial, herbaceous plant. The first year it grows as

Scarlet Gilia

a leafy rosette on the surface of the soil. The second year it sends up an 8-40" tall leafy flowering stem, completes its life cycle, and dies. Occasionally it survives to bloom another season before dying. The leaves have many narrow, pinnately arranged segments and a skunky odor when crushed. The flower petals are joined into a slender tube about ½–¾" long that abruptly expands like a trumpet, into 5 sharply pointed lobes. The plants have many showy flowers that vary in color from scarlet to pale pink, speckled with white.

April–August.

Habitat/Range: Rocky slopes and banks, in dry meadows, and open dry forests from the valleys to the montane and lower subalpine zones.

Comments: The name *Ipomopsis* comes from Greek words meaning "striking appearance." It was formerly included in the genus *Gilia* but is now distinguished as a separate genus having well-developed leaves on the flowering stem and trumpet-shaped flowers. The morphologic distinction is supported by genetic differences as well.

KELSEYA
Kelseya uniflora (Wats.) Rydb.
Rose Family (Rosaceae)

Description: *Kelseya* appears mosslike, clinging in dense cushions to limestone walls. The cushions consist of densely crowded woody branches that are less than 3" long. The branches are covered with dense, overlapping, gray-green leaves. The leaves are small (less than ¼" long) and are covered with soft, silky, straight hair. The flowers are pink and tinged with purple and have 5 sepals, 5 petals, 10 stamens, and 3 styles. The pink stamens and styles are longer than the petals and protrude conspicuously from the flower.

April–early July.

Habitat/Range: Limestone rock crevices in a few localities in the mountains east of the Continental Divide in MT, in south-central ID, and in the Bighorn Mountains of WY; endemic to the Central Rocky Mountains.

Comments: *Kelseya* is unique in the rose family; it is the only species in the genus *Kelseya*. It was named in honor of an early Montana botanist, Reverend Francis D. Kelsey (1849–1905).

Kelseya

Kelsey discovered this plant in 1888, northeast of Helena, Montana. One hundred years later, in 1988, the newly formed Montana Native Plant Society adopted Kelseya as its mascot plant and the title of its newsletter, the *Kelseya*.

Woods Rose

WOODS ROSE
Rosa woodsii Lindl.
Rose Family (Rosaceae)

Description: Wild roses are easily recognized by their light pink to deep reddish flowers and spiny foliage, much like domestic roses. The native roses of the Central Rocky Mountains look very much alike, with 5 green sepals, 5 showy petals, and many stamens. Woods rose has stout (often curved) prickles below the stipules, where the leaf is attached to the stem. The stem is also prickly on the internodes (between the leaf attachments), but these are much smaller than the prickles below the stipules. The compound leaves have 5–9 leaflets with coarse teeth. The flowers are clustered in groups on the ends of the lateral branches. The styles are persistent on the mature red fruit, which is the well-known rose hip.

May–July.

Habitat/Range: Moist, riparian habitats along streams, ponds, and ravines from the plains to the montane forests.

Comments: Wild rose is the floral emblem of Alberta, North Dakota, and New York. People around the world have used roses for food, medicine, and cosmetics. The hips are an excellent source of vitamin C and make a fine tea, syrup, or jam. The Native Americans of Nevada used woods rose as a beverage, a cure for colds, to stimulate urination, and as a dressing for sores, burns, and wounds. The Cheyenne people used woods rose tea to treat diarrhea, stomach trouble, and as an eyewash.

SUBALPINE SPIRAEA
Spiraea splendens Baum. ex Koch
(Also *Spiraea densiflora* Nutt. ex T. & G.)
Rose Family (Rosaceae)

Description: Subalpine spiraea is a low shrub, less than 40" tall. It has alternately arranged, toothed leaves and a flat-topped flower arrangement much like shiny-leaved spiraea (*S. betulifolia*). However, subalpine spiraea has bright pink to rose-red flowers, while shiny-leaved spiraea has white flowers.

June–August.

Habitat/Range: Along streams and the shores of lakes and ponds or in moist woods.

Comments: *Spiraea* comes from a Greek word meaning "coil" or "wreath," in reference to the use of the plants for garlands. Herbalists value the medicinal properties of meadowsweet (*Spiraea ulmaria*), a European species, and steeplebush meadowsweet (*Spiraea tomentosa*), from eastern North America. These herbs are used for relieving pain and inflammation, much the same as aspirin. However, unlike aspirin,

Subalpine Spiraea

meadowsweet is soothing to the mucus membranes of the stomach and digestive tract. Native Americans used various *Spiraea* species to treat diarrhea and dysentery and to stop bleeding.

ELEPHANT'S HEAD
Pedicularis groenlandica Retz.
Figwort Family (Scrophulariaceae)

Elephant's Head

Description: If you look closely at an individual flower you will see the head of a little pink elephant, complete with a long, curved trunk and large, drooping ears. The leaves are fernlike, with individual leaf segments arranged opposite each other along the main leaf axis. The elephant's trunk is the upturned beak (to ½" long) of the upper flower petal. The petals are pink to purple or almost red.

June–August.

Habitat/Range: Wet meadows and along stream banks and lakeshores of the montane forest and subalpine forests.

Comments: Elephant's head, and other species of *Pedicularis,* are used by herbalists as sedative herbs. The close resemblance of the flower to a pink elephant is amazingly humorous. The flowers are pollinated by bees, as are most of the lousewort (*Pedicularis*) species in the Central Rocky Mountains. The wet meadow habitat of elephant's head is rich in floral diversity, and the fragile ecological balance of wet meadow habitat is more vulnerable to disturbance than the adjacent uplands. It deserves special care.

RED AND ORANGE FLOWERS

Rocky Mountain Paintbrush

You may need to also check the blue/purple and pink sections of this book if the flower you are searching for is not found here.

ORANGE MOUNTAIN-DANDELION
Agoseris aurantiaca (Hook.) Greene
Aster Family (Asteraceae)

Description: The bright orange flowers of orange mountain-dandelion distinguish it from

Orange Mountain-Dandelion

the yellow-flowered common dandelion (*Taraxacum officianale*) and other species of *Agoseris*. All basal leaves, heads with only ray flowers, milky juice, and the beaked fruit (achene) are characteristics that all of these plants have in common. The beak is a slender projection from the end of the achene, which connects it with the pappus, which is the "parachute" that carries the achene aloft in the wind. The outer bracts of common dandelion are much shorter than the inner bracts, and they turn backward away from the flower head, while the bracts (modified leaves that enclose the base of the flower head) of *Agoseris* species are all similar in size and project forward toward the flower head.

June–August.

Habitat/Range: Moist to somewhat dry meadows, on open slopes, in forest openings, and in open woods from the valleys and foothills to the upper subalpine forests.

Comments: *Agoseris* is named for the Greek *aix* (goat) and *seris* (chicory). Although they are similar in appearance, mountain-dandelions are native plants and thus do not deserve the scornful reputation of the introduced common dandelion, the infamous lawn weed.

STRAWBERRY BLIGHT
Chenopodium capitatum (L.) Asch.
Goosefoot Family (Chenopodiaceae)

Description: Strawberry blight is distinctive with its triangular or arrowhead-shaped leaves. The tiny, bright red flowers are arranged in dense, fleshy clusters. These round, red floral clusters are attached to the end of the branches and in the leaf axils. They not only look like strawberries, but when they are pressed between the fingers, a red juice is rendered, much like an overripe strawberry.

June–August.

Habitat/Range: Open, disturbed soils in full sun; especially abundant following a forest fire.

Comments: *Chenopodium* is Greek for "goose foot," in reference to the shape of the leaves of many species. The leaves of strawberry blight and the related lamb's quarter (*C. album*) are

Strawberry Blight

edible and rich in vitamins and minerals. This species is a fine potherb, tasting much like spinach. Also like spinach, it is high in oxalic acid. If eaten in excess, it can interfere with calcium absorption and form a precipitate of calcium oxalate that may interfere with kidney function.

Wood Lily

WOOD LILY
Lilium philadelphicum L.
(Also *Lilium umbellatum* Pursh)
Lily Family (Liliaceae)

Description: Wood lily is among the largest and showiest of the wildflowers in the Central Rocky Mountains. The six bright orange to brick-red flower petals are 2–3" long and up to ¼" wide, tapering to a long, narrow basal segment. The lower ⅓ of the petal blades is purple spotted. The stamens are also purple. The stems are erect and about 1–2' tall or taller. The long, narrow leaves are usually arranged alternately, except the uppermost leaves, which form a whorl below the flower. There is usually only 1 flower per stem, but sometimes up to 3.

June–August.

Habitat/Range: Clay-loam soils (derived from limestone or other alkaline rocks) in meadows, grasslands, and open woodlands from the prairies, valleys, and foothills into the montane forests, often in aspen groves.

Comments: Wood lily was collected by Meriwether Lewis near the Mandan villages of present-day North Dakota, where the Lewis and Clark Expedition spent the winter of 1804–1805. The native Dakota people used this plant to treat the bites of the brown spider, chewing or pulverizing the flowers before applying them to the bites. This was said to relieve the inflammation and swelling immediately.

Scarlet Globe Mallow

SCARLET GLOBE MALLOW
Sphaeralcea coccinea (Pursh) Rydb.
(Also *Cristaria coccinea* Pursh)
Mallow Family (Malvaceae)

Description: Scarlet globe mallow is a low plant (less than 8" tall) that spreads by underground stems. The leaves are small and deeply lobed or cut into smaller segments. The upper surface of the leaves is yellowish green, while the lower surface is more grayish. The flowers are arranged in short racemes on the end of the branches. The lower portions of the filaments are joined together into a tube; this is a characteristic of the mallow family. The flower petals are about ⅔" long and bright orange to rusty red in color.

June–July.

Habitat/Range: Dry prairies of the Great Plains, and west in the dry mountain valleys of the Rocky Mountains as far as the Bitterroot Valley, MT; Bannock County, ID; and parts of OR.

Comments: The name *Sphaeralcea* comes from the Greek words *sphaera* (sphere) and *alcea* (mallow), probably in reference to the round or globular fruit of these mallows. *Coccinea* means "scarlet." Meriwether Lewis collected this plant on July 20, 1806, in the plains along the Marias River in Montana. Scarlet globe mallow has slimy, viscous sap that can stick to skin or mucous membranes and thus provide a protective coating. The native Dakota people chewed the plant and applied it to inflamed sores and wounds as a salve. It was said to cool the inflammation and promote healing.

Foxtail Barley

FOXTAIL BARLEY
Hordeum jubatum L.
Grass Family (Poaceae)

Description: The showy, red-tinted spikes (flower heads) of this common grass do look a bit like the tails of red foxes. In foxtail barley, the flowers are arranged in spikes that are attached directly to the rachis (main flower axis) without a pedicel (flower stalk). The red color is from the awns, which are the long, thin, hairlike bristles arising from the tip of the tiny floral structures of the grass. The awns of foxtail barley are ½–2½" long. Foxtail barley grows in dense bunches up to 2' tall. Like other grasses, the leaves of foxtail barley are 2-ranked, bending away from the stem in opposite directions when viewed from above. A leaf consists of a sheath that clasps the round stem, and a blade. The blades of foxtail barley are usually rolled in from the edge, rather than flat. The flower spikes bend downward on the flexible flowering stems, as if nodding off to sleep.

June–August.

Habitat/Range: Disturbed soils of sandbars, blowouts, roadsides, and heavily grazed areas, both wet and dry, from the plains and valleys up to the montane forest zone.

Comments: "The silken rye" was the name that Meriwether Lewis applied to this lovely grass. On June 25, 1805, Lewis wrote in his journal: "there is a species of wild rye which is now heading it rises to the hight of 18 or 20 inches, the beard is remarkably fine and soft it is a very handsome grass the culm is jointed and is in every rispect the wild rye in minuture." On that day the Lewis and Clark Expedition was engaged in portaging the Great Falls of the Missouri River in present-day Montana. Although it is a native grass, it is often considered a weed by ranchers and farmers because it invades cultivated soil and the awns tend to stick in the hair of animals, irritating their skin.

James' Saxifrage

JAMES' SAXIFRAGE
Telesonix jamesii (Torr.) Raf.
(Also *Saxifraga jamesii* Torr.)
(Also *Boykinia heucheriformis* Rosend.)
Saxifrage Family (Saxifragaceae)

Description: Both the sepals and petals of James' saxifrage are red or reddish in color. The ovary has two carpels. The two separate styles are joined together at the base, just before the attachment with the ovary. The leaves are kidney-shaped and alternate, with blunt or rounded teeth on the margin. The plants are covered with glandular hairs.

July–August.

Habitat/Range: Rocky crevices and talus, often on limestone or other calcareous rocks in the montane and subalpine forests.

Comments: The Idaho Conservation Data Center (1994) listed James' saxifrage with an M (monitor) ranking. Rare plants such as James' saxifrage contribute much to the richness of the flora of the Central Rocky Mountains, and they deserve special monitoring and care.

ROCKY MOUNTAIN PAINTBRUSH
Castilleja covilleana Henderson
Figwort Family (Scrophulariaceae)

Description: Rocky Mountain paintbrush is shorter (less than 1' high) than scarlet paintbrush (*C. miniata*). The leaves and bracts are deeply divided into 3–7 divergent, narrow lobes. The leaves, bracts, and stems are covered with long, silky hair. The bracts and sepals are brightly colored, from red to scarlet or occasionally yellow to orange. The upper petal lip of the flower is shorter than the tube and is not noticeable beyond the bracts.

June–August.

Habitat/Range: Mountain slopes and summits of central ID and adjacent MT; endemic to the Central Rocky Mountains—not known from anywhere else on earth. In Montana it is listed as a species of special concern by the Montana Natural Heritage program, and a "sensitive species" by the USDA Forest Service in the Northern Region.

Rocky Mountain Paintbrush

Comments: The name *covilleana* is derived from the Latin *co-* (with, together) and *villi* (long, soft, straight hair), in reference to the villous hair that covers most of this plant.

Scarlet Paintbrush

SCARLET PAINTBRUSH
Castilleja miniata Dougl.
Figwort Family (Scrophulariaceae)

Description: Scarlet paintbrush is rather tall as paintbrushes go, reaching a height of about 1–3'. The leaves are all entire (not lobed) and narrowly lance-shaped. The brightly colored bracts are lance-shaped and deeply divided into 1 or 2 pairs of lateral lobes, beginning from the middle of the bract or lower. Both bracts and sepals are bright red, scarlet, or crimson to red-orange. The upper lip petal is rather long (½– ¾") and extends well beyond the sepals and bracts. In the Central Rocky Mountains scarlet paintbrush often hybridizes with splitleaf paintbrush (*C. rhexifolia*) and other species, resulting in intermediates that complicate identification even for professional botanists.

July–August.

Habitat/Range: Moist meadows and along streams from midmontane forests to the subalpine.

Comments: Paintbrushes are partially parasitic plants, deriving some of their nutrients and water from nearby host plants. The paintbrush plant attaches to the roots of a host plant by means of a short side branch of a root, which is formed specifically for that purpose. The paintbrush exerts a negative pressure on the host's tissues, pulling water and nutrients into its own roots and stems. During a drought, paintbrushes will often appear more healthy than their withered neighbors, which are doubly stressed.

Yellow Flowers

Arrowleaf Balsamroot

This section includes flowers from a bright, golden yellow to a pale, cream color. Some flowers have mixed colors, such as yellow and red or yellow and brown. If the predominant color is yellow, they are included here. Many species with yellow flowers also have green or orange flower variations. You may need to check those sections of this book if the flower you are searching for is not found here.

Skunkbush Sumac

SKUNKBUSH SUMAC
Rhus aromatica Aiton
(Also *Rhus trilobata* Nutt.)
Sumac Family (Anacardiaceae)

Description: The flowers of the skunkbush sumac are arranged in a spike, with the flowers attached directly to the stem, without a flower stalk. The fruit is a red, berrylike drupe (a fleshy, one-seeded fruit) with a glandular coating and a single pit. The leaves are compound, with 3 oaklike leaflets. In the fall these leaves turn a dull, mottled orange-red. The plants often grow into stiff and densely branched shrub masses that are rounded or hemispherical in shape. These shrubs are great cover for rabbits and small birds. *May–June.*

Habitat/Range: Warm and dry, often rocky slopes in the foothills and river breaks.

Comments: Although closely related to poison ivy and poison oak (*Toxicodendron* species), skunkbush sumac and its cousin, smooth sumac (*Rhus glabra*), are actually edible, medicinal species. The glandular coating on the dry, red berries of skunkbush sumac has a pleasant lemony flavor, either consumed raw or made into a beverage by placing in hot or cold water. Various Native American tribes powdered the dried berries and applied them to smallpox and other open sores. Others boiled the fruit, using the tea to treat bleeding, tuberculosis, and kidney disorders. The leaves were dried and smoked. The twigs were used to prepare a yellow dye.

Western Poison Ivy

WESTERN POISON IVY
Toxicodendron rydbergii (Small ex Rydb.)
  Greene
(Also *Rhus rydbergii* Small)
Sumac Family (Anacardiaceae)

Description: Western poison ivy is a low shrub (less than 5' tall), without the climbing habit or aerial roots of the more eastern poison ivy vine (*T. radicans*). The stems are hairy and stand upright. The compound leaf has 3 smooth, green leaflets that turn bright red in the fall. The leaf margin has a few irregular teeth. The flowers are small and cream colored with purplish veins. The fruit is a globe-shaped, cream-colored, berrylike drupe. The cluster of "berries" remains on the plants long after the foliage has fallen, and often throughout the winter.

May–June.

Habitat/Range: Along rivers and streams in the valleys, foothills, and lower mountains, mostly below 5,000 feet of elevation in MT.

Comments: The name *Toxicodendron* is from the Greek *toxikos* (poisonous) and *dendron* (tree). The well-known itchy rash that results from handling these plants comes from a poison in the resin ducts throughout the plant. Fortunately, only about half the population is sensitive to an average contact with the poison, but unfortunately, there is no known cure if you are sensitive. There are cases of people being repeatedly reinfected with the rash by handling clothing or garden implements that have been contaminated with the poisonous resin. Firefighters have been infected by breathing the ash of burning plants.

American Thorough-Wax

AMERICAN THOROUGH-WAX
Bupleurum americanum Coult. & Rose
Parsley Family (Apiaceae)

Description: This is the only species of the parsley family in the Central Rocky Mountains with all simple, entire leaves. Heart-leaved alexanders (*Zizia aptera*) has simple basal leaves and compound stem leaves. The many other species in the family have leaves that are all compound, with several to many leaflets. Both basal and stem leaves of American thorough-wax are simple, long and narrow (6" long and ½" wide), with prominent parallel veins and a smooth margin (no teeth). The flowers are arranged compound umbel, typical of the parsley family. A whorl of well-developed leafy bractlets is present at the common point where the individual flower stalks join together, and another whorl of leafy bracts (an involucre) is found at the point where the rays join the main stem. The flower clusters are dense and bright yellow or sometimes purple lined with yellow.

July–August.

Habitat/Range: Rock outcrops, open grasslands, dry meadows from the foothills to the highest alpine summits; most common east of the Continental Divide, but it does cross the divide into western MT, western WY, and east-central ID.

Comments: *Bupleurum* comes from an ancient Greek word meaning "ox rib." In Chinese herbology *Bupleurum* is among the most important herbs because it is used to treat liver disturbances, a common problem. It is also used to treat chronic bronchitis, muscle and joint pain, and serious abdominal diseases. Some modern western herbalists believe that *B. americanum* is almost identical with the Chinese herb in its herbal constituents. They value the herb as a bile stimulant, antihistamatic, and for lowering blood pressure and fevers.

Cous Biscuit-Root

COUS BISCUIT-ROOT
Lomatium cous (Wats.) Coult. & Rose
Parsley Family (Apiaceae)

Description: Cous biscuit-root is a low plant (less than 14" tall) with compound leaves that are finely dissected into many small segments. The plants are usually smooth (hairless). The leaves tend to wither and turn yellow as the fruit matures. The flowers are yellow and are arranged in compound umbels, typical of the parsley family. A whorl of well-developed leafy bracts is present at the common point where the individual flower stalks join together. These bracts are relatively large and broadly egg-shaped or spatula-shaped, the key to correct identification. There are no leafy bracts at the point where the rays join the main stem. The rays are of various lengths; some long, some short. The fruit has a narrow, thin margin (lateral wing), which is typical of the genus *Lomatium*.

April–June.

Habitat/Range: Rocky slopes, grasslands, and sagebrush steppes from the valleys, foothills, and montane forests to subalpine parks and alpine turf above timberline.

Comments: According to the Lewis and Clark journals, "cous" or "cows" is the "Chopunnish" (Nez Perce) Indian name for this plant, while the Walla Walla people referred to the plant as "shappellel." Meriwether Lewis collected a specimen of the plant on April 29, 1806, near what we now call the Walla Walla River, in Washington. On the specimen's label, his description reads: "An umbelliferous plant of the root of which the Wallowallows make a kind of bread." This plant was among the most important food plants of the native people of the region, and it was mentioned often as a food and trade item in the Lewis and Clark journals. On May 10, 1806, in the "Chopunnish" village of "broken Arm," William Clark wrote in his journal, "the noise of their women pounding the cows root remind me of a nail factory."

HEART-LEAVED ALEXANDERS
Zizia aptera (Gray) Fern.
Parsley Family (Apiaceae)

Description: This is an erect plant 8–24" tall. It has simple, heart-shaped basal leaves and compound stem leaves with 3 leaflets. All the leaves are smooth (hairless) and have teeth on the margin. The bright yellow flowers are arranged in a compound umbel. There are no leafy bracts where the rays join together, and only a few inconspicuous bracts at the common point of the individual flower stalks.

May–July.

Habitat/Range: Moist to wet meadows and along stream banks; eastern WA, OR, southeastern ID.

Comments: *Zizia* was named for Johann Ziz (1779–1829). Native Americans used the related golden alexanders (*Z. aurea*) to treat fevers, head congestion, and headache. The plants are reported to have toxic properties, causing vomiting.

Heart-Leaved Alexanders

SEEP-SPRING ARNICA
Arnica longifolia D. C. Eaton
Aster Family (Asteraceae)

Description: Seep-spring arnica spreads by underground stems and forms dense colonies, often to the exclusion of other plant species. The leafy stems are 1–3' tall. Some stems are topped by several flower heads, while many other stems are without flowers. The leaves are in 5–7 pairs arranged opposite each other on the stem, with no true basal leaves. The foliage is covered with short hairs, rough to the touch, and sometimes with a glandular secretion. The leafy bracts that ring the base of the flower head are sharply pointed. The flower heads have yellow rays surrounding the yellow disk flowers.

July–September.

Habitat/Range: Seeps, springs, moist cliffs, and talus of open subalpine slopes up to timberline.

Comments: Several species of *Arnica* have long been used by herbalists in treating bruises, joint inflammation, sore muscles, and sprains externally. They are believed to be effective in fighting bacteria and increasing circulation to speed healing. Taken internally, however, arnica has been known to cause severe gastroenteritis.

Seep-Spring Arnica

Hairy Arnica

HAIRY ARNICA
Arnica mollis Hook.
Aster Family (Asteraceae)

Description: Hairy arnica plants are similar in size, creeping habit, and wet habitat to seep-spring arnica. However, hairy arnica has fewer pairs of stem leaves (3–4) and larger heads, with the disk sometimes up to 1½" wide. The leaves of hairy arnica are more than 2" wide and thus broader than those of seep-spring arnica. The lower leaves of hairy arnica are usually the largest. The entire plant is covered with short, glandular hairs. The flower heads are solitary and both ray and disk flowers are yellow.

July–early September.

Habitat/Range: Along streams, seeps, and springs of the upper montane and subalpine zones to timberline.

Comments: In the Central Rocky Mountains hairy arnica often shares its streamside habitat with monkey-flowers (*Mimulus* species) and columbines (*Aquilegia* species) in showy riparian gardens.

NODDING ARNICA
Arnica parryi A. Gray
Aster Family (Asteraceae)

Description: Before blooming, the young heads of nodding arnica hang sadly downward on limp stems. As blooming progresses the heads turn up happily to smile at the sky. The heads have only tiny, yellow disk flowers and lack any rays, at least in the phase that occurs in the Central Rocky Mountains. The stems are usually solitary and 8–24" tall. The leaves are lance-shaped, up to 8" long and 2½" wide; they are well developed at the base but are much smaller on the stem. The plants are hairy throughout and glandular on the upper portion.

June–August.

Habitat/Range: Open woods and meadows from the foothills to the subalpine forest.

Comments: *Arnica parryi* is named in honor of Charles Parry, an early botanist who collected the first botanical specimen of this species in Colorado in 1861.

Nodding Arnica

Arrowleaf Balsamroot

ARROWLEAF BALSAMROOT
Balsamorhiza sagitatta (Pursh) Nutt.
Aster Family (Asteraceae)

Description: Arrowleaf balsamroot is most often confused with mule's-ears (*Wyethia* species). However, arrowleaf balsamroot has well-developed leaves that originate at the base of the plant and very small, reduced, ones (if any) on the flowering stem. Mule's-ears have large, well-developed leaves on the flowering stem. The leaves and bracts of arrowleaf balsamroot appear silvery due to dense, white, feltlike hair that covers the plant surface, especially early in the season. The leaves are large (up to 12" long and 6" wide) and shaped like giant arrowheads. The yellow flower heads are solitary on the long stems and resemble sunflowers.

April–July.

Habitat/Range: Dry soil of grasslands, sagebrush steppes, and dry forests from the valleys through the montane forests.

Comments: *Balsamorhiza* (balsamroot) is named for the sap in its large woody root, which has the aroma and texture of balsam fir pitch. Native Americans used the root for treating various diseases, swellings, and insect bites, and as a fumigant. They also relied on all parts of the plant for food. The seeds were ground into flour and made into a kind of bread. Meriwether Lewis of the Lewis and Clark Expedition collected a specimen of balsamroot on April 14, 1806, near present-day White Salmon, Washington. The specimen label and journal entries for that day document the native people gathering "parcels of the Stems" and eating the stems of balsamroot "without any preparation." Modern herbalists rely on the plant to fight infections, loosen phlegm, and boost the immune system.

RUBBER RABBIT-BRUSH
Chrysothamnus nauseosus (Pall.) Britt.
Aster Family (Asteraceae)

Rubber Rabbit-Brush

Description: Rubber rabbit-brush is a medium-sized woody shrub, 1–5' tall. The flower heads have only disk flowers: about 5 tiny yellow flowers per head. The bracts surrounding the base of each flower head are arranged in 5 vertical ranks, overlapping like shingles on a roof. The stems and twigs are covered with a fine, white, feltlike hair. The leaves are narrow (⅛"), linear, and 1–3" long.

August–October.

Habitat/Range: Dry, open places in the grasslands, sagebrush steppes, and dry forests from the plains and valleys up to the montane forest zone.

Comments: The name *Chrysothamnus* is derived from the Greek roots *chrys* (golden yellow) and *thamn* (bush). *Nauseosus* implies that the plant produces sickness or nausea. Jackrabbits often hide under the cover of rabbit-brush to conceal themselves from the watchful eyes of the golden eagle soaring overhead. The Shoshone people of Nevada used the plant to stop diarrhea and as a remedy for coughs and colds. The Cheyenne used it to relieve itching and treat smallpox.

OREGON SUNSHINE
Eriophyllum lanatum (Pursh) Forbes
(Also *Actinella lanata* Pursh)
Aster Family (Asteraceae)

Description: Oregon sunshine is a perennial, herbaceous plant 4–24" tall. The stems and foliage are covered with densely matted, soft, woolly hair that gives the plant a gray-green appearance. The leaves may be entire, lobed, or deeply cleft into several narrow segments. The flower heads have bright, golden yellow ray and disk flowers. The woolly bracts that surround the base of each flower head are all about the same size. They form a single vertical row, but they overlap horizontally.

May–August.

Habitat/Range: Open, dry places from the valleys to above timberline.

Comments: *Eriophyllum* was derived from the Greek *erion* (wool) and *phyllon* (foliage). *Lanatum* is from the Latin *lanatus* (woolly). Woolly foliage is a major characteristic distin-

Oregon Sunshine

guishing this plant. Meriwether Lewis collected a specimen of this species on June 6, 1806, along the high uplands of the "Kooskooskee" (Clearwater) River, near "Camp Chopunnish," or present-day Kamiah, Idaho.

Blanket Flower

BLANKET FLOWER
Gaillardia aristata Pursh
Aster Family (Asteraceae)

Description: Blanket flower has multicolored flower heads. The showy ray flowers (on the outer margin of the flower head) are yellow, becoming purplish toward the base. The disk flowers (in the center of the flower head) are purple to brownish purple and covered with woolly hair. The tips of the ray petals are deeply divided into 3 prominent lobes. The leafy bracts (around the base of the flower head) taper to a long point. The stems, leaves, and bracts are covered with long, loose hairs. The shape of the leaf is variable, from entire to toothed and deeply cut into lobes.

May–September.

Habitat/Range: Dry soil of the prairies and dry meadows from the valleys and foothills to the montane forests.

Comments: *Gaillardia* was named in honor of the French botanist Gaillard de Marentonneau. The name *aristata* comes from the Latin word *arista* (awn; bristle) in reference to the bristles on the single-seeded fruit (achene). The species was first named and described to science by Frederick Pursh in 1814, from a specimen collected by Meriwether Lewis on July 7, 1806. On this day Lewis crossed the Continental Divide between the Blackfoot River and the Dearborn River on his return trip to the Great Falls of the Missouri, during the famous Lewis and Clark Expedition. Native American people used blanket flower medicinally for intestinal infections, skin disorders, and kidney problems, and as an eyewash and for preparing nose drops.

CURLY-CUP GUMWEED
Grindelia squarrosa (Pursh) Dunal
Aster Family (Asteraceae)

Description: Curly-cup gumweed is aptly named. The leaves and flower bracts have glands that exude an aromatic resin that is sticky or gummy to the touch. The numerous green, leafy bracts form a cup at the base of the flower head.

Curly-Cup Gumweed

Each bract curls downward at its slender tip. The flower heads consist of numerous (25–40) yellow ray flowers surrounding the yellow disk. The middle and upper leaves clasp the stem.

July–September.

Habitat/Range: Dry soil, often in areas that have been disturbed, from the valleys into the dry montane forest zone.

Comments: *Grindelia* was named in honor of the Russian botanist David Grindel (1776–1836). *Squarrosa* is a botanical term describing the downward curling tips of the bracts. Native American people used this plant to treat a variety of serious illnesses including smallpox, measles, pneumonia, and venereal disease. It was also used as a remedy for coughs and for bladder, kidney, stomach, and liver trouble. Externally it was applied as an antiseptic wash or poultice on various wounds and swellings and to relieve the itching of poison ivy rash. Picking up on the Indian use of the plant for treating poison ivy, commercially available lotions have been developed from *Grindelia*.

CUSHION GOLDENWEED
Haplopappus acaulis (Nutt.) Gray
Aster Family (Asteraceae)

Description: Cushion goldenweed is most likely to be confused with stemless hymenoxys (*Hymenoxys acaulis*). Both are low, mat-forming cushion plants with a single, bright yellow flower head on an apparently leafless stem. However, the ray petals of cushion goldenweed are entire, without the 3-lobed tip of stemless hymenoxys. Cushion goldenweed has a few small leaves on the flowering stem, while the stem of hymenoxys is entirely naked. Cushion goldenweed has sharply pointed leafy bracts that surround the base of the flower head. These bracts are papery, somewhat darker toward the tip, but not green or leaflike, as those of hymenoxys.

May–August.

Habitat/Range: Dry, open, windswept places from the valleys and foothills to the alpine fellfield.

Comments: Cushion goldenweed often grows with cushion milkvetch (*Astragalus kentrophyta*)

Cushion Goldenweed

and other mat-forming plants. These species are at home in the low elevation desert badlands and in the windswept alpine fellfield on top of the highest mountains. This shows how these seemingly unrelated habitats actually have much in common. Both are dry habitats causing high water losses and stress on plants; both have short growing seasons—conditions in which cushion plants thrive.

SHRUBBY GOLDENWEED
Haplopappus suffruticosus (Nutt.) Gray
Aster Family (Asteraceae)

Description: This is a woody shrub, low growing (less than 16") but not mat forming. The
leaves have a peculiar curly or wavy margin and
are sticky with glandular hairs. There are only
3–8 widely spaced yellow ray flowers around the
margin of the yellow flower disk; this is unusual
for such a large and striking flower head. The
bracts that surround the flower head are glandular and are found in two forms: the outer
bracts are longer and more leaflike than the inner
bracts.

July–August.

Habitat/Range: Rocky places in the high
mountains, near or above the timberline; western WY, southwestern MT, ID, OR.

Shrubby Goldenweed

Comments: *Haplopappus* is named for the
Greek words *haplous* (simple) and *pappos* (seed
down).

MOUNTAIN LITTLE SUNFLOWER
Helianthella uniflora (Nutt.) T. & G.
Aster Family (Asteraceae)

Description: Mountain little sunflower is generally smaller than nodding little sunflower, only
8–40" tall. The leaves are arranged opposite on
the stem, except for the topmost leaves, which
are alternate. The leaves of this species are more
narrowly lanceolate than nodding little
sunflower's, having only a single pair of prominent lateral veins. The flower heads are more
erect. The leafy bracts around the base of the
flower head are stiff and narrowly lance-shaped.
The ray petals are bright yellow, surrounding a
yellow disk.

June–August.

Habitat/Range: Open hillsides and sparsely
timbered slopes from the valleys and sagebrush
foothills to the subalpine forests; central and
eastern WA and OR, central ID, and west and
central MT and WY.

Comments: The plant is named *uniflora* because
there is usually only one flower head per stem.
Mountain little sunflower is abundant in the
Yellowstone ecosystem, often growing with
lupine (*Lupinus* species); together they cover the
hillsides with bright yellow and blue.

Mountain Little Sunflower

Nodding Little Sunflower

NODDING LITTLE SUNFLOWER

Helianthella quinquenervis (Hook.) Gray
Aster Family (Asteraceae)

Description: Nodding little sunflower is a large perennial plant 2–5' tall. The leaves are arranged in pairs on opposite sides of the stem. There are 2 pairs of prominent lateral veins on each leaf. The flower heads are turned downward or to the side. The leafy bracts that line the base of the flower head are soft and broadly lance-shaped. The pale yellow ray petals surround a yellow disk. Little sunflowers (*Helianthella* species) have a single-seeded fruit, called an achene, that is thin and strongly flattened, with a thin-edged margin. The stiff awns or bristles on the end of the achene remain intact, even as the fruit matures. In contrast, true sunflowers (*Helianthus* species) have thick, quadrangular achenes with awns that quickly fall away.

June–August.

Habitat/Range: Meadows and open forests from the foothills to the subalpine forests; southeastern OR, central ID, southwestern MT, WY.

Comments: *Quinquenervis* means "five-nerved." The leaves have a midvein and four prominent lateral veins, or five veins (nerves) total. Aspen sunflower is another common name for this species, because it favors the rich soil and moisture found in aspen groves. Nectar is secreted from the margins of the floral bracts of aspen sunflower, from before flowering until just before seed dispersal. This nectar attracts ants, which often swarm the plants at rather high densities. These ants aggressively defend the plant and its sweet nectar from other insects that try to visit the plants, including flies that attempt to lay their eggs on the flowers. If successful, the fly larvae would eat the sunflower seeds; thus, aspen sunflower benefits from the behavior of the ants, and the relationship is mutually beneficial.

Common Sunflower

COMMON SUNFLOWER
Helianthus annuus L.
Aster Family (Asteraceae)

Description: Common sunflower is a large (1–7' tall), coarse, annual herbaceous plant. The leaves are 4–16" long and 2–8" wide and are alternately arranged (except the lowest). The leaf and stem surface is rough and hairy. The flower head consists of yellow ray flowers surrounding a reddish brown disk. The green bracts around the base of the flower head are egg-shaped, narrowing to a long, sharp tip. The fruit is a 1-seeded achene, familiar to everyone as a "sunflower seed." The hull of the achene is quadrangular in cross section, with 2 stiff awns or bristles on the end that tend to fall off as the seed matures.

June–September.

Habitat/Range: Open, disturbed places in the prairies, valleys, and foothills.

Comments: The name *Helianthus* comes from the Greek word *helios* (sun) and *anthos* (flower), literally "sunflower." The flower disks usually face the sun and follow its path across the sky. Common sunflower has been cultivated for its edible seed and oil since pre-Columbian times. For example, it is known to have been cultivated by the Arikara, Mandan, and Hidatsa people of North Dakota. The sunflower plant was also used medicinally for respiratory ailments, burns, and rattlesnake bites.

ALPINE SUNFLOWER
Hymenoxys grandiflora (T. & G.) Parker
(Also *Rydbergia grandiflora* Greene)
Aster Family (Asteraceae)

Description: Alpine sunflower is distinctive in the alpine tundra, producing by far the largest

Alpine Sunflower

flower heads to be found there. The showy yellow flower heads are 2–4" in diameter and usually solitary on the stems. The petals of the ray flowers have a 3-lobed tip. The plants are about 8" tall. The leaves are deeply cut into several narrow, linear segments and are covered with cobwebby or woolly hair.

June–August.

Habitat/Range: Subalpine and alpine tundra.

Comments: *Hymenoxys* is from the Greek words *hymen* (membrane) and *oxys* (sharp), which describe the sharply pointed scales on top of the ovary or fruit. It is sometimes called "sun god" and "old-man-of-the-mountain". Alpine sunflower grows as an inconspicuous vegetative plant for many years while storing the energy to produce the huge flower heads. When enough energy is stored, the plant blooms and dies. Picking these beautiful wildflowers would deny this plant its only opportunity to reproduce.

PINEAPPLE WEED
Matricaria matricarioides (Less.) Porter
(Also *Chamomilla suaveolens* Ryd.)
Aster Family (Asteraceae)

Description: This little annual is more likely to be noticed from its pleasant pineapple aroma than from its inconspicuous flowers. The plants are 2–12" tall. The numerous leaves are divided into fine, short, linear segments. The flower disk is conical and yellowish green, but without ray flowers. The bracts around the base of the flower head have a thin, translucent margin.

May–August.

Habitat/Range: Disturbed places, such as ground squirrel mounds, roadsides, and cracks in the pavement.

Comments: *Matricaria* is from the Latin *mater* (womb), a name given by early herbalists to medicinal plants of gynecological value. This plant is related to German chamomile (*Matricaria recutita*) and may have similar properties. Herbalists use chamomile for indigestion, insomnia, tension, insect bites, and eczema. Meriwether Lewis collected a specimen of this plant along the "Kooskoosky" (Clearwater) River

Pineapple Weed

of Idaho in the spring of 1806, while among the Nez Perce Indians. Flathead Indian people used pineapple weed for colds, upset stomach, as an aid at childbirth, and to relieve menstrual cramps. They also used it to help preserve meat. Its fragrant flower heads were used to line babies' cradles or were strung as a necklace.

PRAIRIE CONEFLOWER
Ratibida columnifera (Nutt.) Woot. & Standl.
Aster Family (Asteraceae)

Description: Prairie coneflower usually has bright yellow ray flowers surrounding a dark brown, long, column-shaped disk. Less often the rays are partially or entirely purple in color. The distinctive column, or narrow, thimble-shaped disk, can be as much as 1¾" long or as little as ½" long. The rays are few in number (3–7), broad, and turn downward away from the disk. The leaves are deeply cut into numerous linear or lance-shaped segments.

June–September.

Habitat/Range: Dry plains, grasslands, and sagebrush steppe of the valleys and foothills; MT, WY, southeastern ID.

Comments: Native American people of the plains (Lakota, Dakota, Cheyenne) used the prairie coneflower variously as a tealike beverage and medicinally to cure stomachache, headache, chest pains, wounds, rattlesnake bites, and poison ivy rash.

Prairie Coneflower

TWICE-HAIRY BUTTERWEED
Senecio fuscatus Hayek
Aster Family (Asteraceae)

Twice-Hairy Butterweed

Description: This plant is called "twice-hairy" because it has long, cobwebby hairs underlain by short, dense, flat-lying hairs that cover the leaves, stems, and flower head bracts. The bracts that surround the base of the flower head are arranged in a single row, narrowly lance-shaped, and purplish toward the tip. The plants are only 4–8" tall with broad leaves that often taper toward the base. The flower heads have yellowish rays surrounding a rather large (½–¾" wide) orange disk.

July–August.

Habitat/Range: Alpine meadows above treeline in the Beartooth Mountains of MT and WY.

Comments: *Senecio* comes from the Latin word *senex* (old man), probably because of the abundant white hair in species such as twice-hairy butterweed. The name *fuscatus* comes from a Latin word meaning "darkened," likely in reference to the darkened tips of the flower head bracts, typical of plants in the genus *Senecio*. Groundsel is another common name for plants in this genus.

Tall Butterweed

TALL BUTTERWEED
Senecio serra Hook.
Aster Family (Asteraceae)

Description: As the name suggests, these herbaceous plants are 2–6' tall or taller. The stems are crowded with leaves from top to bottom. The leaves are 3–6" long and narrow (½–1½" wide) and taper toward the base. The margin of the leaf is lined with fine, sharp teeth, like a saw. The leaves have numerous lateral veins. The abundant yellow flower heads are crowded on the top of the stems. The leafy bracts that surround the base of each flower head form a single row of uniform length, touching at the margins, but not overlapping, like a ring of little green soldiers. There are often a few shorter bracts, irregularly spaced, in a second outer whorl. The pointed tip of each bract is often black or at least darker than the body.

June–September.

Habitat/Range: Moist meadows, along streams, and in other moist forest openings from the valleys and foothills to the subalpine forests; western MT, ID, eastern WA, OR, WY.

Comments: *Senecio* is one of the largest genera of plants worldwide, with over twelve hundred species. They are widely distributed geographically and highly diverse in habitat and life form, including trees and shrubs. There are fifty or more species of *Senecio* in North America. At least seven of the species studied contain toxic alkaloids that are poisonous if eaten, causing acute liver damage to livestock and humans. Species of *Senecio* have also caused cell mutations, birth defects, and liver tumors when consumed.

MEADOW GOLDENROD
Solidago canadensis L.
Aster Family (Asteraceae)

Description: Meadow goldenrod is a large, leafy herbaceous plant 1–6' tall or taller. The stems have dense, short hairs throughout, or at least above the middle of the plant. The lance-shaped leaves are 2–6" long and less than 1" wide, and they are well distributed on the stems (not basal). The leaf margin is often toothed, at least on the upper portion. There are 3 main nerves or veins from the base of the leaf. Numerous small, yellow flower heads crowd the ends of the stems. Surrounding the base of each small flower head are long, thin overlapping bracts of varying lengths. *July–October.*

Habitat/Range: Wet meadows and swales, along streams, and in moist open woods from the valleys to the subalpine forest.

Comments: The Omaha Indians correlated the blooming of goldenrod with the ripening of corn, reminding them to return home for the harvest. The plants often develop large, round insect galls on their stems. These galls have been used by some Native Americans, when mixed with prickly ash, to make a tea for kidney problems.

Meadow Goldenrod

Showy Goldeneye

SHOWY GOLDENEYE
Viguiera multiflora (Nutt.) Blake
Aster Family (Asteraceae)

Description: Showy goldeneye is one of many sunflowerlike, perennial herbaceous plants. The flower heads have yellow rays surrounding a yellow to brown disk. The disk is medium-sized (½" wide or less). The leafy bracts around the base of the flower head are in 2 or 3 overlapping rows. Each bract is narrowly lance-shaped. The "sunflower seed" fruit (achene) is naked, lacking the awns or pappus bristles that are present on the achene of most plants in the aster family. The leaves are opposite, except for the uppermost leaves on the stem, which are alternate. The plants are 1–4' tall.

July–September.

Habitat/Range: Dry hillsides and disturbed places from the valleys to the montane forests; southwestern MT, southeastern ID, WY.

Comments: *Viguiera* was named in honor of Alexandre Viguier (1790–1867), a physician and botanist from Montpellier, France.

Missouri Goldenrod

MISSOURI GOLDENROD
Solidago missouriensis Nutt.
Aster Family (Asteraceae)

Description: Missouri goldenrod has its larger leaves at the base of the stem, with the upper leaves becoming progressively smaller. The lower leaves taper to a narrow petiole (leaf stalk), while the upper leaves are attached directly to the main stem of the plant, without a petiole. The leaves and stems are smooth, without the copious hair or white (glaucous) coating of related species. Plants are intermediate in height (8–36"). The yellow flower heads are small and densely arranged on the end of the stems.

June–October.

Habitat/Range: Grasslands and forest openings from the plains and valleys up into parks of the lower subalpine forest.

Comments: The name *Solidago* is derived from the Latin words *solidus* and *ago* (to make whole) because of the healing value of some species. Herbalists have used species of goldenrod for its astringent and drying properties to stop bleeding and close wounds, to reduce phlegm, and as an anti-inflammatory agent for the mucous membranes. Other reported herbal medicinal applications include use as a urinary antiseptic, a sedative, and for reducing blood pressure. It has also been cooked as a green vegetable.

Yellow Mule's-Ears

YELLOW MULE'S-EARS

Wyethia amplexicaulis Nutt.
Aster Family (Asteraceae)

Description: The leaves of this distinctive plant are like the ears of a mule in both shape and size. The plants are smooth, with a resinous, varnishlike, shiny surface that gives the plants a distinctive aroma. Yellow mule's-ears lacks the dense hairs present on the leaves and stems of the similar and closely related balsamroot (*Balsamorhiza* species) and white mule's ears (*Wyethia helianthoides*). The dark green leaves are present both at the base of the plant and along the flowering stem. The large flower heads are sunflower-like, with bright yellow rays surrounding a yellow disk.

May–June.

Habitat/Range: Meadows and open forests from the foothills and montane forests to the lower subalpine forests; central WA, ID, western MT, WY, OR.

Comments: *Wyethia* is named in honor of Nathaniel Wyeth (1802–1856), an early explorer and plant collector. In the Central Rocky Mountains, yellow mule's-ears often hybridizes with white mule's-ears, producing an intermediate plant with pale yellowish flowers and sparse hairs. The Shoshone people of Nevada used the resinous roots of yellow mule's-ears as a poultice on swellings, in a solution to promote vomiting, and in compound preparations with other herbs to treat syphilis and measles.

Creeping Oregongrape

CREEPING OREGONGRAPE
Berberis repens Lindl.
(Also *Mahonia repens* (Lindl.) G. Don)
Barberry Family (Berberidaceae)

Description: Creeping Oregongrape is a low shrub, about 1' tall, with distinctive hollylike evergreen leaves. It is called "creeping" because it spreads by runners or horizontal stems below the soil surface, which makes it resistant to damage by fire. The leaves are less than twice as long as broad, with small spines on the margin. The bright yellow flowers give way to a grapelike cluster of purple berries with a whitish coating. In the fall, some of the leaves often turn bright red, orange, or bronze.

April–June.

Habitat/Range: Dry forests and on open slopes from the foothills to the lower subalpine forests.

Comments: The tart berries make a refreshing, lemonade-like drink and fine jelly or wine. The yellow inner bark was used widely by Native Americans as a yellow dye and a medicine with many applications. It was believed to be especially useful for easing child delivery, healing wounds, fighting infections, and treating venereal disease and kidney problems. The alkaloid berberine, isolated from the yellow sap, has been shown to have antibiotic activity against a broad spectrum of bacteria and protozoa. Modern herbalists use the herb for fevers, inflammations, infections, indigestion, and liver and gall bladder disorders.

Thin-Leaved Alder

THIN-LEAVED ALDER
Alnus incana (L.) Moench
Birch Family (Betulaceae)

Description: Thin-leaved alder is a tall shrub (6–36' high) that sometimes appears treelike. The leaf margin is doubly sawtoothed, having both large and small teeth. In winter, the buds are identifiable by the distinctive stalk at the base and the blunt or rounded tip. The bark is smooth and gray on young stems, but scaly and reddish brown on old trunks. The flowers are unisexual, with male flowers and female flowers borne in separate flower arrangements, but both appearing on the same (monoecious) plant. The yellow male flowers hang downward in long, spiraled clusters, or catkins. The female flowers are borne in stout, egg-shaped woody catkins, which look like miniature pinecones. These "cones" remain intact on the shrub through the winter.

Late March–June.

Habitat/Range: Streams, rivers, and the shores of ponds and lakes from the valleys to the subalpine forests.

Comments: Alder bark is loaded with tannin, a chemical compound valuable for tanning hides. A reddish brown to orange dye is also obtained from the bark. Some Native Americans used it to dye moccasins, feathers, and even their hair. An astringent, medicinal tea was made from the bark. Herbalists consider this tea useful internally for improving digestion and externally for poison ivy rash and insect bites. Medical research has isolated compounds from one species of alder that shows promise in cancer chemotherapy.

YELLOWSTONE DRABA
Draba incerta Pays.
Mustard Family (Brassicaceae)

Yellowstone Draba

Description: Yellowstone draba is a ground-hugging cushion plant. The leaves are widest above the middle, tapering toward the base. The leaf surface has branched, comblike hairs (visible with a 10x hand lens). The flowering stems are leafless, varying greatly in height, from ½"– 20" tall. The bright yellow flowers have 4 sepals and 4 petals, typical of the mustard family. The fruit is a flattened, egg-shaped pod, often covered with short, stiff hairs.

June–July.

Habitat/Range: Subalpine and alpine summits, ridges, and fellfields.

Comments: *Draba* is from a Latin word meaning "acrid." The sap of drabas, and many others in the mustard family, is sharp and somewhat caustic to the tongue, mucous membranes, and even the skin. There are at least a dozen species of yellow-flowered cushion drabas in the Central Rocky Mountains. Identification of species is a technical task requiring careful study.

ROUGH WALLFLOWER
Erysimum asperum (Nutt.) DC.
Mustard Family (Brassicaceae)

Description: This is an erect plant, 8–40" tall, often with a single stem, but sometimes having a few branches. A cluster of spreading or radiating leaves grows from the base of the plant, while numerous alternate leaves also line the stems. The margin of the leaves varies widely from entire to toothed. A cluster of bright yellow to orange flowers is arranged in a raceme on the end of the stem. The flowers are rather large, each with 4 petals as much as 1" long. The fruit is a long, narrow pod, 1–4" long, which reaches upward.

May–July.

Habitat/Range: Plains and valleys up to timberline.

Comments: Wallflowers and other members of the mustard family have long been used medicinally in a mustard plaster poultice for relief of bronchial congestion. Left on too long, the poultice can cause serious skin blistering.

Rough Wallflower

COMMON TWINPOD
Physaria didymocarpa (Hook.) Gray
Mustard Family (Brassicaceae)

Description: The large, inflated, 2-lobed pods of the mature fruit attract attention to this plant, which might otherwise be seen as just another yellow-flowered mustard plant. The pods and foliage are covered with star-shaped hairs (as seen under a 10x lens). The style is persistent in the notch between the 2 balloonlike lobes of the pods. The plant has numerous basal leaves that form a rosette at the ground surface. These basal leaves are broad, blunt, and somewhat angular and gradually taper to a narrow leaf base. The leaves on the flowering stem are small and narrow in comparison.

June–August.

Habitat/Range: Rocky, gravelly soil of shaley slopes, talus, or "badlands" from the valleys to the montane forests and alpine fellfields; MT, WY, central and eastern ID, southeastern WA.

Comments: The name *Physaria* comes from the Greek word *physa* (bellows), a perfect descrip-

Common Twinpod

tion of the inflated fruit of this plant. *Didymocarpa* is Greek for "double fruit," describing the two lobes of the pods.

CUSHION NIPPLE CACTUS
Coryphantha missouriensis (Sweet)
   Britt. & Rose
Cactus Family (Cactaceae)

Description: These low, spiny cacti are globe-shaped, with spines that radiate from the ends of small, nipplelike tubercles (areoles) that protrude from the main body of the cactus. The flowers have numerous lance-shaped petals that are greenish yellow, sometimes with a reddish tinge. The fruit is almost round and quite red.

June–July.

Habitat/Range: Plains, valleys, and foothills; MT and ID, especially along the Salmon River.

Comments: *Coryphantha* is derived from the Greek words *koryphe* (cluster) and *anthos* (flower). A second species of nipple cactus in our area (*C. vivipara*) has reddish purple flowers and green fruit. The shamans of the Tarahumara people of Mexico are said to use a species of *Coryphantha* in their ceremonies. Another *Coryphantha* species is reported as a hallucinogen in Mexico. Chemical studies have isolated several alkaloids from these cacti.

Cushion Nipple Cactus

Plains Prickly Pear

PLAINS PRICKLY PEAR
Opuntia polyacantha Haw.
Cactus Family (Cactaceae)

Description: The long spines and flattened, blue-green pads of plains prickly pear are familiar to anyone who has had the misfortune to step on one. As if the sharp, long spines are not trouble enough, the plants are also armed with a ring of tiny, hairlike barbs (glochids) at the base of the larger spines. These tiny barbs look harmless, but once touched they penetrate the skin and refuse to let go. However, the beautiful flowers of prickly pear more than compensate for the dreaded spines. The flowers are large, up to 3" or more, with numerous yellow to red petals. The fruit is a pear-shaped berry, dry and very spiny, unlike the juicy "tunas" of some southwestern species of prickly pear.

May–June.

Habitat/Range: Dry grasslands from the plains into the foothills, canyons, and montane forests.

Comments: This was the most dreaded plant encountered by the Lewis and Clark Expedition (1804–1806). On July 15, 1805, while ascending the Missouri River near the mouth of the Smith River, Lewis noted in his journal: "the prickly pear is now in full blume and forms one of the beauties as well as the greatest pest of the plains."

BEARBERRY HONEYSUCKLE
Lonicera involucrata (Rich.) Banks ex Spreng.
Honeysuckle Family (Caprifoliaceae)

Description: Bearberry honeysuckle is a medium-sized shrub (2–6' tall or taller) with opposite leaves. The leaves are entire (without lobes or teeth), egg-shaped, and with a pointed tip. The yellow flowers are borne in pairs from the leaf axils. Immediately underneath the twin flowers are 2 sets of conspicuous, green to purple tinged, leafy bracts. As the fruit develops, the bracts also continue to grow and deepen in color. The mature fruits are pairs of round, black berries with large purplish red bracts just beneath.

Habitat/Range: Stream sides, in moist woods, or in shrub thickets.

Comments: *Lonicera* is named in honor of Adam Lonitzer (1528–1586), a German botanist. The name *involucrata* refers to the prominent bracts or involucre of bearberry honeysuckle. Utah honeysuckle (*L. utahensis*) is also common in the Central Rocky Mountains. It lacks the prominent bracts of bearberry honeysuckle, has bright red twin berries, and its leaves have a rounded tip.

Bearberry Honeysuckle

Whitlow Wort

WHITLOW WORT
Paronychia sessiliflora Nutt.
Pink Family (Caryophyllaceae)

Description: The dense, yellow-green leaves of Whitlow wort form cushionlike mats up to 8" wide and 2" or more thick. The leaves are awl-shaped, sharply pointed, and densely crowded on the stems. The flowers have 5 brownish yellow sepals, 5 stamens, and 1 style. The style is divided into 2 segments in the upper fourth of its length. There are no petals.

June–August.

Habitat/Range: Plains to alpine.

Comments: *Paronychia* comes from a Greek word that refers to an inflammation under the fingernail, which this herb was supposed to treat. *Sessiliflora* means that the flowers are sessile—that is, attached directly to the main stems without a flower stalk (pedicel). "Wort" is a term for an herbaceous (nonwoody) plant.

LANCE-LEAVED STONECROP
Sedum lanceolatum Torr.
Stonecrop Family (Crassulaceae)

Lance-Leaved Stonecrop

Description: Lance-leaved stonecrop is a small (less than 12" tall), herbaceous plant with succulent leaves that are round in cross section. The leaves are lance-shaped, tapering from midlength to the tip. At the base of the plants there are short, sterile shoots that are densely crowded with clusters of radiating basal leaves. The leaves on the flowering stem are alternately arranged and often fall off by the time of flowering. The flowers are like yellow stars, with 5 sepals and 5 sharply pointed petals.

June–August.

Habitat/Range: Rocky and gravelly soils from sea level to the subalpine forests.

Comments: The name *Sedum* is derived from the Latin *sedeo* (to sit) probably because of its low growing habit. Native people in the Arctic eat the rose-colored stonecrop that grows there. Some edible plant enthusiasts also relish the juicy leaves of lance-leaved stonecrop. However, some people find it unpalatable.

YELLOW MOUNTAIN HEATHER
Phyllodoce glanduliflora (Hook.) Coville
Heath Family (Ericaceae)

Description: Yellow mountain heather is a dwarf, woody shrub, 4–16" tall, with evergreen leaves that look like coniferous fir needles. The plants often form mats that appear to be coniferous krummholz. However, the yellowish flowers at the end of the branches announce that it is not a conifer. The flowers are narrowly contracted at the mouth, like an urn or pitcher. The outer surfaces of the sepals, petals, and young stems are covered with short glandular hairs. The fruit is a capsule that splits open along the lines of the partitions.

July–August.

Habitat/Range: Alpine.

Comments: *Phyllodoce* is from the Greek name for a sea nymph. Yellow mountain heather often hybridizes with the closely related red mountain heather (*P. empetriformis*), producing plants with intermediate characteristics of both parents.

Yellow Mountain Heather

Silverberry

SILVERBERRY
Elaeagnus commutata Bernh.
Oleaster Family (Elaeagnaceae)

Description: Silverberry is a 3–12' tall or taller shrub with silvery leaves and fruit. It spreads by rootstocks, often forming dense colonies. The numerous stems are flexible, like a willow's, and without the thorns of the similar Russian olive and silver buffalo-berry. The surfaces of the leaves and fruit are covered with small branlike or star-shaped scales, visible with a hand lens. The dry, berrylike fruit is round to egg-shaped, rather large (½" long), and persistent on the branches, in clusters, throughout the winter. The flowers are perfect (include both male and female structures) and consisting of 4 rather showy yellow sepals (but no true petals), 4 stamens, and a pistil. The flowers emit a pleasant lemony fragrance when in bloom that is apparent for some distance from the plants.

May–July.

Habitat/Range: Foothills, montane forest zone; MT, WY, and the upper Snake River plain in ID.

Comments: *Elaeagnus* comes from the Greek *elaia* (olive) and *agnos* (willow). Russian olive (*E. angustifolia*) is a closely related species introduced from Europe. Russian olive is a thorny tree (up to 30' tall) with narrow leaves that are 3–8 times as long as wide. In contrast, silverberry is a nonthorny native shrub with wider leaves that are only 1½–3 times as long as wide. Russian olive is an insidious threat to the native vegetation along the streams and rivers of the West, where it has been planted for windbreaks. It is gradually crowding out the native riparian trees and shrubs, slowly but surely establishing dense monoculture stands of Russian olive.

Silver Buffalo-Berry

SILVER BUFFALO-BERRY
Shepherdia argentea (Pursh) Nutt.
Oleaster Family (Elaeagnaceae)

Description: The thorn-tipped stems, silvery opposite leaves, and bright red berries of silver buffalo-berry set it apart from other native shrubs of the Central Rocky Mountains. The silvery leaves may be confused with silverberry and Russian olive, but both of these shrubs have alternately arranged leaves and a dry, silvery fruit. Silver buffalo-berry is a rigidly branched, 6–18' tall shrub. The surface of the leaves and young twigs are covered with small branlike or star-shaped scales, visible with a hand lens. The plants are dioecious, with unisexual male and female flowers on separate plants. The male flowers consist of 4 sepals and 8 stamens. The female flowers consist of 4 sepals and a pistil. The flowers usually bloom before the leaves have expanded. The fruit is a round, red, juicy berry. *April–June.*

Habitat/Range: Streams, moist coulee bottoms, and woody draws in the plains and foothills; MT, WY, and southeastern OR.

Comments: *Shepherdia* was named for the English botanist, John Shepherd (1764–1836). The first scientific specimen of silver buffalo-berry was collected by Meriwether Lewis in September 1804 on the banks of the Missouri River at the mouth of the Niobrara River, which is on the border between present-day Nebraska and South Dakota. It is called buffalo-berry because the dried berries were often mixed with dried buffalo meat to from a staple food of the Native American people of the Great Plains. The ripe berries are best gathered after the first frost, when sugar content is highest. The finest wild jam (in my opinion) is made from wild buffalo-berries; it is tart with a unique flavor.

Pinedrops

PINEDROPS

Pterospora andromedea Nutt.
Heath Family (Ericaceae)

Description: The tall reddish brown stems of pinedrops stand like stoic sentinels of the forest floor, unbranched and leafless. The live stems are 12–40" tall, fleshy, and covered with glandular hairs. The dried stalks of dead plants remain standing for a year or more. The plants grow singly or in clusters but are seldom abundant. They have no need for chlorophyll for food production. They are nourished by fungi which they parasitize for nutrients. The fungi obtain these nutrients in turn from live trees, or the decaying wood, needles, and twigs that make up the organic layer in the soil. The upper half of the stem supports a raceme of yellowish flowers that hang downward from recurved pedicels (bent-back flower stalks). The petals are united into an urn-shaped tube with 5 small, spreading lobes at the apex.

June–August.

Habitat/Range: Well developed, deep humus layers in the forest floor of coniferous forests in montane and subalpine zones.

Comments: *Pterospora* means "winged-seed." *Andromedea* is named for the character in Greek mythology. Andromeda was the daughter of Cassiopeia and Cepheus, the queen and king of Ethiopia. To punish the boastful Cassiopeia, the sea gods had Andromeda chained to a rock at the edge of the sea, where she could be attacked by Cetus the whale. However, Perseus intervened and turned Cetus into stone by showing him the head of Medusa, thus saving the distressed Andromeda. In autumn's night sky, Andromeda is a constellation that lies near Cassiopeia and Cetus with Perseus nearby as if rushing to save her.

Leafy Spurge

LEAFY SPURGE
Euphorbia esula L.
Spurge Family (Euphorbiaceae)

Description: Leafy spurge is a long-lived perennial, herbaceous plant, 1–3' tall, with deep, heavy rootstocks. It is vigorously colonial, spreading laterally and forming dense communities, often excluding other plants in its way. The leaves are 1–3" long and narrow (less than ½" wide). When the leaves or stems are broken, a white, milklike sap exudes from the wound. There are no true petals or sepals; instead, heart-shaped, petal-like, yellowish green leafy bracts serve the purpose. The ovary is borne on the end of a stalk, so that it protrudes from the upper bracts. The flowers are arranged in umbels, with rays that start from a common point and divide into 2 rays at the junction of a leafy bract. This pattern is repeated several times until the stamens and ovary are reached at the top of the arrangement.

May–August.

Habitat/Range: Introduced noxious weed; disturbed soils of roadsides and fields, spreading from there into natural plant communities of the valleys, foothills, and montane forests.

Comments: *Euphorbia* is named in honor of Euphorbus, the physician of King Juba II, from the ancient kingdom of Numidia in North Africa. This is one of the largest and most diversified genera of plants in the world, with over a thousand species, mostly tropical. Poinsettia and snow-on-the-mountain are popular ornamental plants in the genus. Twelve native species of spurge occur in the Pacific Northwest. Leafy spurges and other *Euphorbias* are known to be poisonous. Cattle and horses seem to be affected by the toxic properties of spurge more than sheep, which readily eat leafy spurge.

Wild Licorice

WILD LICORICE
Glycyrrhiza lepidota Pursh
Bean Family (Fabaceae)

Description: The first thing you are likely to notice about this plant is the fruit: a bur, densely armed with hooked prickles, that grabs your clothing and clings to your socks. The reddish brown pods develop in clusters in the leaf axils. They remain on the plants throughout the season or at least until hitching a ride on a passing animal. The dense arrangement of flowers, which precedes the fruit, is yellowish to off-white in color, sometimes with a faint purple tinge. The petals are irregular and include the banner, wings, and keel petals, typical of the bean family. The leaves are compound, made up of numerous pairs of lance-shaped leaflets along the leaf axis (rachis). The stems, foliage, and flower arrangement are covered with round or stalked glands that are often sticky to the touch.

The glands on the underside of the leaves appear as tiny dots.

May–July.

Habitat/Range: Moist swales, along stream banks, or on the shores of ponds in the plains, valleys, foothills, and lower montane.

Comments: *Glycyrrhiza* comes from the Greek words *glykys* (sweet) and *rhiza* (root). The licorice traditionally used for medicine and to flavor foods is from Europe (*G. glabra*). Wild licorice is the North American version, which has many of the same properties. While wintering at Fort Clatsop (January 4, 1806), Meriwether Lewis wrote in his journal: "I observe no difference between the liquorice of this country and that common to many parts of the United States . . . the natives roast it in the embers and pound it slightly with a small stick . . . this root when roasted possesses an agreeable flavour not unlike the sweet pittaitoe."

YELLOW SWEETVETCH
Hedysarum sulphurescens Rydb.
Bean Family (Fabaceae)

Description: Yellow sweetvetch develops several leafy stems, 1–2' tall, from a single thick rootstock. The leaves are pinnately compound, with numerous pairs of oval leaflets along the main leaf axis. The pale yellow (or almost white)

Yellow Sweetvetch

flowers are arranged in a raceme of 20–100 flowers that hang downward from the main flower stalk. The irregular flowers are typical of the bean family, having 5 petals: a banner, 2 wings, and a keel. The wing petals of yellow sweetvetch are much shorter than the large keel petal. The fruit is a pod, constricted between the seeds, that forms up to 4 segments.

June–August.

Habitat/Range: Montane and subalpine forests.

Comments: Yellow sweetvetch is most likely to be confused with yellow species of locoweed (*Astragalus* species) or crazyweed (*Oxytropis* species), such as silky crazyweed (*Oxytropis sericea*), which also has yellow to white flowers and pinnately compound leaves. However, the wing petals of locoweed and crazyweed are as long or even longer than the keel petal, and the pods are not constricted between the seeds into distinct segments, as they are in sweetvetch.

SILKY CRAZYWEED
Oxytropis sericea Nutt.
Bean Family (Fabaceae)

Description: Silky crazyweed grows in dense tufts of basal leaves, up to 12" long, from a woody taproot. The leaves are pinnately compound, with 5–10 pairs of leaflets attached to the main leaf axis. Soft, silky hairs cover the surface of the leaflets, giving them a grayish appearance. The numerous (10–30) flowers are arranged in a raceme on the end of a leafless stem 4–10" long. Flower color varies from yellow to white. Each irregular flower has 5 petals: a banner, 2 wings, and a keel. The wings are longer than the keel petal, concealing it. The keel petal is abruptly contracted at the end into a thin, often purple-tipped point. The fruit has a thick, fleshy wall that hardens into a bony pod upon drying.

Mid-May July.

Habitat/Range: Dry grasslands from the prairies, foothills, subalpine forest.

Comments: The name *Oxytropis* comes from the Greek *oxys* (sharp) and *tropis* (keel). The sharp point or beak on the end of the keel petal of the flower is a major characteristic of the

Silky Crazyweed

genus, separating it from the closely related locoweed (*Astragalus* species). Point locoweed is another common name of *Oxytropis*. Silky crazyweed and certain other species of *Oxytropis* and *Astragalus* cause loco poisoning in livestock. Symptoms of loco poisoning include emaciation, trembling of the head, difficulty eating and drinking, listlessness, and death. Affected animals apparently become addicted to locoweed, because they develop the strange behavior of craving and seeking it out, while ignoring good forage.

ROUND-LEAVED GOLDEN-PEA
Thermopsis rhombifolia Nutt. ex Richardson
Bean Family (Fabaceae)

Description: This is a low (6–20" tall), leafy herbaceous plant. The compound leaves have 3 oval leaflets and 2 large, leafy stipules at the base of the leaf attachment. The leafy stems have a raceme arrangement of 7–30 bright yellow flowers on the end. Each irregular flower has a banner, 2 wings, and a keel petal, typical of the bean family. The 10 stamens are distinct, not joined together by their filaments like many plants in the bean family. The fruit is a long, flat pod, which may be curved or straight.

April–June.

Habitat/Range: Plains, foothills, montane forests.

Comments: *Thermopsis* comes from the Greek words *thermos* (lupine) and *opsis* (resemblance), hence one of the common names for this genus, false lupine. It is also called buck bean, yellow bean, golden banner, and buffalo bean. These plants contain several alkaloids, suspected to be

Round-Leaved Golden-Pea

poisonous and to have caused loss of life in cattle, horses, and children who ingest the plants. Although these deaths have not been positively linked to the plant, it would be prudent to avoid eating the pods or any part of round-leaved golden-pea.

GOLDEN SMOKE
Corydalis aurea Willd.
Fumitory Family (Fumariaceae)

Golden Smoke

Description: Golden smoke is a winter annual or biennial up to 20" tall. It germinates in the fall and overwinters as a seedling. In the spring it makes rapid growth, flowers, and dies by the end of the growing season. The foliage consists of compound leaves with many small, linear segments. The leaves appear smoky green because they are covered with a fine, white, powdery substance, which rubs off. The flowers are yellow and quite showy. There are 4 petals, the outer 2 hooded and crested, and the inner 2 joined together at the tip. A long spur, containing nectar, extends backward from the upper (outer) petal.

May–July.

Habitat/Range: Disturbed sites, such as shores of rivers and lakes, road cuts, and forest fires.

Comments: *Corydalis* comes from the Greek word *korydallis* (crested lark); the spurred flower looks like the head of a crested lark. Golden smoke is suspected of being poisonous to livestock, like its close relative fitweed (*C. caseana*). In clinical trials, drugs from some species of *Corydalis* show promise in treating cardiac arrhythmia and venereal disease.

Golden Currant

GOLDEN CURRANT
Ribes aureum Pursh
Currant Family (Grossulariaceae)

Description: Golden currant is a medium-sized (3–9' tall) woody shrub. The leaves are smooth, deeply 3-lobed, and arranged alternately on the stems. The stems are smooth, lacking the prickles of some species of *Ribes*. The flowers are golden yellow. The flower tube (hypanthium) is funnel-shaped and attached to the top of the ovary. Five yellow, petal-like sepals flare from the end of the tube. Attached just inside the mouth of the flower tube are the 5 smaller, true petals and the 5 stamens. The berries vary in color from yellow and orange to red or even black. The bright yellow flowers are among the first to appear along the streams and rivers of the Central Rocky Mountains.

April–May.

Habitat/Range: Streams and rivers of the prairies, foothills, and montane forests.

Comments: The name *Ribes* comes from *ribas,* an Arabic name for the plants. Meriwether Lewis described golden currant in his journal on July 18, 1805, when near the mouth of the Dearborn River: "a great abundance of red yellow perple & black currants and service berries now ripe . . . particularly the yellow currant which I think vastly preferable to those of our gardens." After this, he provided a detailed botanical description that shows how observant and versed in botanical language Lewis was. Lewis' 1805 collection of golden currant is the earliest known botanical collection from Montana, and it is among the over two hundred Lewis specimens now preserved at the Academy of Natural Sciences in Philadelphia.

Common St. John's Wort

COMMON ST. JOHN'S WORT
Hypericum perforatum L.
St. John's Wort Family (Hypericaceae) (Also Clusiaceae)

Description: Common St. John's wort is a perennial, herbaceous plant 1–3' tall that spreads with creeping horizontal stems, both above and below ground. The leaves are opposite, are much longer than wide, and tend to taper toward the base. The surface of the leaf has tiny glandular dots, like pinpricks, that are best seen by holding the leaf up to a light source. Crushing the leaves with your fingers yields a red pigment. The plant has bright yellow flowers clustered on the ends of the stems. The sepals are narrow, 3–5 times longer than wide. The margin of the petals is lined with dots, similar to those on the leaves. The numerous stamens have purple-tipped anthers. There are 3 styles on the ovary, which matures into a 3-beaked capsule.

June–July.

Habitat/Range: Introduced noxious weed; disturbed places, spreading into more natural habitats; most common west of the Continental Divide.

Comments: The name *perforatum* probably refers to the pinhole dots, or perforations, on the leaves and the margin of the petals. Western St. John's wort (*H. formosum*) is a related species that is native to the Central Rocky Mountains at high elevations. It has much broader leaves and sepals than common St. John's wort. Herbalists value St. John's wort for treating depression. It is also use to treat gastritis, ulcers, abrasions, and burns. The main active ingredient, hypericin, can cause photosensitivity and dermatitis in animals, including humans. Livestock feeding on the foliage have developed severe skin lesions, sometimes causing death.

Glacier Lily

GLACIER LILY
Erythronium grandiflorum Pursh
Lily Family (Liliaceae)

Description: Glacier lily is easily recognized by its few (2–4) large, showy, yellow (or white) flowers, with 6 tepals (petals and petal-like sepals) that are abruptly bent backward toward the base. The 6 protruding stamens may have white, yellow, red, or purple anthers. The style is tipped with 3 stigma lobes. There are 2 parallel-veined (unmottled) leaves, 4–8" long, near the base of the stem. The white-flowered glacier lilies of southeastern Washington and adjacent Idaho are the variety *candidum*.

March–August.

Habitat/Range: Foothills, montane and subalpine forests to timberline.

Comments: *Erythronium* comes from the Greek word *erythro* (red), referring to the red flowers of some species. Glacier lily is also known as adder's tongue, trout lily, fawn lily, and dogtooth violet. Glacier lilies bloom as the snow melts in the mountains, following the snow line as it recedes up the slopes. These flowers are so lovely that it would be tempting to plant them in the garden. However, those who have tried have usually failed. It is best to enjoy glacier lilies in their wild habitat.

YELLOW BELL
Fritillaria pudica (Pursh) Sprengel
Lily Family (Liliaceae)

Description: Yellow bell is a small (4–12" tall) perennial, herbaceous plant with erect stems and leaves that develop from a cluster of bulblets. There are 2–8 leaves on the stem. The leaves are about 4" long and narrowly linear in shape. The flowers are yellow to orange when they first bloom, but fade to red or purple as they age. Most plants have but a single flower, but occasionally plants are seen with 2 or 3. The flowers hang downward like a bell. Each flower consists of 6 tepals (the petals and sepals are similar) and the more or less concealed stamen and style within. The fruit is a cylindric to globe-shaped pod.

March–June.

Habitat/Range: Grasslands of the plains, foothills, and montane forests.

Comments: Meriwether Lewis collected a specimen of yellow bell on May 8, 1806, near the Kooskooskee (Clearwater) River in Idaho. On the plant label, Lewis wrote: "The bulb is

Yellow Bell

the shape of a biscuit which the natives eat." The Salish-Kootenai Indians of Montana are said to have mixed yellow bell bulbs with those of the bitterroot, which were ready for digging at the same time. The green seedpods are also known to be edible fresh or boiled. With the decline of wild habitats where these lovely plants can be seen, it is best to leave them for others to enjoy.

BLAZING STAR
Mentzelia laevicaulis (Dougl.) T. & G.
Blazing Star Family (Loasaceae)

Description: The spectacular lemon-yellow flowers of this plant are large (up to 6" in diameter) and very showy. Each flower has 5 lance-shaped petals and numerous yellow stamens.

The 5 outer stamens have expanded, showy filaments, appearing like a set of smaller petals that alternate with the larger, true petals. The fruit is a capsule up to 1½" long. The plants are 9–40" tall, and the stems and foliage are covered with harsh, barbed hairs. The leaves have a deeply wavy margin. The flowers are night blooming, closing during the heat of day.

July–September.

Habitat/Range: Dry, disturbed soil in the valleys and lower mountains.

Comments: *Mentzelia* is named in honor of the German botanist C. Mentzel (1622–1701). The Dakota and Cheyenne people are said to have used blazing star medicinally to treat fevers, earache, rheumatism, arthritis, mumps, measles, and smallpox. It was normally used in combination with other medicinal plants, like purple coneflower (*Echinacea angustifolia*).

Blazing Star

Indian Pond-Lily

INDIAN POND-LILY
Nuphar polysepalum Engelm.
Water-Lily Family (Nymphaeaceae)

Description: We are all familiar with pond-lily, with its leaves floating on the surface of ponds and lakes. The leaves of Indian pond lily are broadly heart-shaped and 4–16" long. The stem reaches as much as 6' down to the roots in the mud. The flowers are bright yellow and quite large, 3–5" in diameter. There are numerous red to purple stamens. The stigma is unusually broad (about 1") and has up to 25 lines that radiate from the center. The fruit is cylindrical, about 3" long, and filled with pelletlike seeds.

May–August.

Habitat/Range: Aquatic; rooted in the muddy bottom of lakes, ponds, and sluggish streams.

Comments: *Nuphar* is derived from an Arabic name for pond-lily. Dr. Ferdinand V. Hayden made the initial scientific botanical collection of Indian pond-lily from a small lake between the Henry's and Snake Forks of the Columbia River, on June 20, 1860, while on the expedition led by Captain William F. Raynolds and guided by mountain man Jim Bridger. The seeds of Indian pond-lily were a staple food of the Klamath Indians, who roasted and ground them into a meal. The roots are edible, too, but only as an emergency food, because of their disagreeable flavor.

Long-Leaved Evening-Primrose

LONG-LEAVED EVENING-PRIMROSE

Camissonia subacaulis (Pursh) Raven
(Also *Oenothera heterantha* Nutt.)
Evening-Primrose Family (Onagraceae)

Description: The 2–12" long leaves of this low plant are all basal, without a leafy stem. The leaves are widest well above the middle, tapering to a narrow basal portion at the petiole (the leaf stem). Some leaves have a few small lobes below the middle of the blade. The flowers are technically stemless, with the ovary attached directly to the leaf axil. Look carefully: the petals and other floral parts are attached to the top of a very slender projection of the ovary, which appears to be a flower stem. The flowers are short-lived, blooming in the morning and wilting later that same day. The 4 yellow petals are about as wide as they are long. The 4 narrow sepals are reflexed away from the petals.

May–July.

Habitat/Range: Moist meadows from the foothills to the subalpine forests; central and eastern WA, OR, ID, MT, and western WY.

Comments: *Camissonia* is named in honor of the German poet and botanist Ludolf Adelbert von Chamisso (1781–1838), who visited California in 1816. Another German botanist, Frederick Pursh, named this plant *Jussieua subacaulis* in 1814, from a specimen collected by Meriwether Lewis. This was most likely the collection by Lewis from "moist ground on the Quamash flats June 14, 1806," today known as Weippe Prairie, Idaho.

Yellow Lady's Slipper

YELLOW LADY'S SLIPPER
Cypripedium calceolus L.
Orchid Family (Orchidaceae)

Description: The distinctly orchid flower of yellow lady's slipper has a large, yellow lip petal, inflated like a pouch. Purplish dots decorate the mouth, or opening of the pouch. A triangular sterile stamen, also yellow with purple dots, hangs down into the pouch opening, pointing the way for insects to enter. The sepals and petals, surrounding the lip, are purplish brown. The lateral petals are long, narrow, and twisted, making up to 3 complete turns. The leaves are broad and taper to a point, with prominent parallel veins. The stems are 8–16" tall, with 3 or 4 alternate leaves and a leafy bract below the solitary flower (or pair of flowers).

May–June.

Habitat/Range: Bogs and other wetlands in low elevation mountains; WA, OR, MT, ID. It is a rare species in the Central Rockies, with small populations widely separated geographically.

Comments: The Orchidaceae is one of the largest plant families, with about five hundred genera and fifteen thousand species worldwide, mostly in tropical forests. *Cypripedium* is named from the Greek *kypris* (Venus) and *pes* (foot), referring to the moccasin-shaped lip. Yellow lady's slipper and other western terrestrial orchids have very specialized habitat and soil requirements, requiring specific soil microorganisms for germination and growth. Because they are rare, and their requirements cannot be duplicated in the garden, they should never be transplanted.

Clustered Broomrape

CLUSTERED BROOMRAPE
Orobanche fasciculata Nutt.
Broomrape Family (Orobanchaceae)

Description: This strange parasitic plant is often overlooked. The stout main plant stems are 2–7" long, but appear much shorter because about ⅔ of their length are buried in the soil. The plants are root parasites, attaching themselves to the roots of various species, especially sagebrush (*Artemisia* species). Since they get their nutrients from the host plant, they have no need for photosynthesis. Hence, the leaves are vestigial: small and bractlike, without chlorophyll. There are 4–10 flower stalks (pedicels) attached to each stem where the bractlike leaves join (in the leaf axis). Each pedicel bears a single flower, yellowish to dull red with purple lines. The petal tube is curved and funnel-shaped with 5 lobes. The sepals are likewise tubular with lobes about the same length as the tube, or shorter.

April–August.

Habitat/Range: Lowlands, foothills, and montane forests.

Comments: *Orobanche* comes from the Greek words *orobos* (vetch) and *anchein* (to choke). It's interesting to note how botanists have applied human values and judgments in naming these parasitic plants, giving the impression that they are plants of violence, raping or choking their hosts. Native American people of Nevada were reported to use broomrape plants for both food and medicine.

Subalpine Buttercup

SUBALPINE BUTTERCUP
Ranunculus eschscholtzii Schlecht.
Buttercup Family (Ranunculaceae)

Description: Subalpine buttercup is a widely variable species with 6 varieties. It has smooth, shiny green leaves with 3 deep lobes. The leaf segments are sometimes lobed again once or twice. The leaves are mostly basal, with the few leaves and/or leafy bracts on the flowering stem reduced in size. The stems are 2–8" tall with 1–3 flowers each. The flowering stems are smooth (hairless). The flowers usually have 5 sepals and 5 petals. The bright yellow petals have a smooth nectary scale at the base. Stamens and pistils are numerous.

June–August.

Habitat/Range: Rocky slopes and moist meadows from subalpine forests up to the alpine summits. They are often found along the margins of receding snowbanks on the lee, or sheltered, side of mountain ridges.

Comments: *Ranunculus* is from the Latin *rana* (frog) and *unculus* (little), likely named because of the wet habitat of many species. Buttercups have acrid juice that can blister or even ulcerate the skin, especially the mucous membranes. Do not put any part of these plants in your mouth, and keep them away from children. Clinical trials have shown the juice to be active against a broad spectrum of bacteria. Species of buttercup have been used in folk herbal medicine to treat abrasions, toothache, rheumatism, hemorrhoids, and perineal tears.

YELLOW COLUMBINE
Aquilegia flavescens S. Watson
Buttercup Family (Ranunculaccae)

Description: Columbine flowers are easily identified by their 5 showy, spurred petals and 5 showy, petal-like sepals. The spurs of yellow columbine are curved inward but not hooked. The sepals are yellow, often tinged with pink (or entirely pink in the variety *miniana*). The petals have cream-colored blades and yellow spurs. The leaves are mostly basal and compound, with 3 sets of 3 (that is, 9) leaflets per leaf. Leaves and/or leafy bracts on the flowering stem are much reduced, both in size and in the number of leaflets. The stems are 8–30" tall.

June–early August.

Habitat/Range: Moist mountain meadows, streams, and canyon bottoms; montane, subalpine, alpine.

Yellow Columbine

Comments: The derivation of *Aquilegia* is disputed. Some say it is derived from the Latin *aqua* (water) and *legere* (to draw), possibly because of its affinity for streamside habitats. Others believe that it is derived from the Latin word *aquila* (eagle) because of the resemblance of the spurs to the talons of an eagle. Columbine is from the Latin *columbinus* (dovelike). If the spurs are viewed as the heads of 5 doves, and the petal blades as their wings, then a columbine flower does resemble 5 doves taking flight. Thus, the columbine can be seen as a symbol of war (the eagle) or of peace (the dove).

ALPINE IVESIA
Ivesia gordonii (Hook.) T. & G.
Rose Family (Rosaceae)

Description: Like alpine avens, this is a perennial, herbaceous plant with pinnately compound basal leaves with many segments, and a few,

Alpine Ivesia

small stem leaves. However, the style of alpine ivesia is attached to the ovary below the summit and falls off as the fruit matures. The fruit is a smooth, beakless achene. The yellow petals are shaped like a spatula and are smaller than the triangular to lance-shaped sepals. The yellow flowers are numerous and are crowded into headlike clusters on the ends of the stems.

June–August.

Habitat/Range: Montane forests and alpine tundra; eastern WA and OR, ID, southwestern MT, western WY.

Comments: The origin of the name *Ivesia* is disputed. One source says it was named in honor of Joseph Christmas Ives (1828–1868), an explorer and officer in the U.S. Army Corps of Topographical Engineers. Ives led the Colorado Exploring Expedition of 1857–1858. Another source claims that it was named for Dr. Eli Ives (1779–1861), an American physician and botanist.

ALPINE AVENS
Geum rossii (R. Br.) Ser.
(Also *Acomastylis rossii* (R. Br.) Greene)
Rose Family (Rosaceae)

Description: Alpine avens is a perennial, herbaceous plant with pinnately compound basal leaves with many narrow segments. The leaves on the flowering stem are much smaller than the basal leaves. *Geum* is distinguished from similar herbs in the rose family by having flowers with a style that arises from the top of the ovary, rather than the base or side. The style of

Alpine Avens

alpine avens is straight and continues to develop as the petals fall and the fruit forms. The mature style is the smooth beak of the single-seeded fruit (achene) and is about the same length. (You will need a hand lens to view these tiny plant parts.) The flowering stems are graced with 1–4 yellow flowers. The flowers have numerous stamens and pistils that vary from few to many. The broad, yellow petals are short-lived. When they fall away, the triangular sepals remain, giving the appearance of a completely different flower.

June–August.

Habitat/Range: Subalpine meadows and alpine tundra.

Comments: *Geum rossii* is named in honor of James C. Ross, an Arctic and Antarctic explorer of the 1800s. The type specimen for the species was collected in 1820 on Melville Island, Northwest Territories, during W. E. Parry's first voyage. Melville Island is in the Arctic Ocean, less than a thousand miles from the North Pole. *Geum* species are astringent herbs valued by herbalists for treating dysentery and for closing and healing cuts and abrasions.

GLOBEFLOWER
Trollius albiflorus (A. Gray) Rydberg
(Also *Trollius laxus* Salisb. var. *albiflorus*
    A.Gray)
Buttercup Family (Ranunculaceae)

Description: The flowers of globeflower are pale yellow as they begin to open but fade to creamy white in full flower. The flowering stems are smooth (hairless), with alternately arranged leaves having short stalks. The basal leaves have long stalks that flare out at the base, clasping the stems. All the leaves are deeply divided into several segments, which are in turn lobed and toothed. The plants are 4–16" tall.

May–August.

Habitat/Range: Wet meadows, swamplands, and stream sides from the montane and subalpine forests to the alpine.

Comments: *Trollius* comes from the German word *trollblume* (globeflower). Globeflower is often confused with marsh-marigold (*Caltha leptosepala*), with which it often co-occurs.

Globeflower

However, the leaves of marsh-marigold are heart-shaped and not divided into segments. In the Bighorn Mountains of Wyoming and south through Colorado, globeflower may be mistaken for the similar subalpine windflower (*Anemone narcissiflora*). However, this species has a hairy stem with a whorl of leafy bracts below the flower, both features missing from globeflower. Globeflower has acrid juice that can blister the skin, similar in that respect to its close relatives the buttercups.

Shrubby Cinquefoil

SHRUBBY CINQUEFOIL

Pentaphylloides fruticosa (L.) Schwarz
(Also *Potentilla fruticosa* L.)
Rose Family (Rosaceae)

Description: This low (1–3' high) shrub, with yellow flowers, is popular in ornamental landscaping. The leaves are compound, with 5 pinnately arranged leaflets. The leaf stalk has prominent stipules at the base. The leaves and stipules are clothed in long, silky hair that give them a bluish green hue. Shreddy, reddish brown bark hangs loosely from the otherwise smooth stems. Individual flowers grow from the leaf axils along the stem, while groups of 3–7 flowers are arranged at the tip. The flowers have 5 petals and numerous stamens and pistils.

Mid-June–August.

Habitat/Range: Wet meadows to dry rocky slopes and open woods from foothills up to subalpine and alpine meadows.

Comments: *Pentaphylloides* is derived from the Greek *penta* (five) and *phylloides* (leaved) for the foliage with 5 leaflets. This genus of shrubs was separated from *Potentilla*, which now includes only herbaceous species. A number of cultivars of this species have been developed by horticulturists for ornamental planting. Herbalists use this, and the closely related *Potentilla* species, as an astringent herb, useful for inflammatory conditions such as diarrhea, gum or throat soreness, poison ivy rash, and sunburn.

Tall Cinquefoil

TALL CINQUEFOIL
Potentilla arguta Pursh
Rose Family (Rosaceae)

Description: Glandular hairs cover the leaves and stems of this perennial herb. If you touch or grasp the foliage, the aromatic fluid from the glands sticks to your fingers. The stems are usually 16–32" in height. The flowering stems are stiffly erect, forming a narrow and densely clustered flower arrangement. A similar species, sticky cinquefoil (*P. glandulosa*), has stems 16" or less high, and a more open flower arrangement. The basal leaves of tall cinquefoil are compound, with 5–9 toothed leaflets pinnately arranged in pairs on the leafstalk. Leaves on the stems are few and much smaller than the basal leaves. The flowers are dull yellow to creamy white, with 5 sepals, 5 petals, and many stamens and pistils. Viewing one of the tiny pistils with a hand lens reveals that the style is attached to the ovary below the middle.

June–August.

Habitat/Range: Meadows and open woods from the valleys to the subalpine forests.

Comments: *Potentilla* is from the Latin *potens* (powerful), probably because of the potent medicinal properties of some of the herbs in this genus. *Potentilla* has a high tannin content, making it very astringent and anti-inflammatory. Herbalists use it to treat diarrhea and various sores and inflammatory conditions of the intestinal tract and mucous membranes.

Bitterbrush

BITTERBRUSH
Purshia tridentata (Pursh) DC.
Rose Family (Rosaceae)

Description: This woody shrub is densely and rigidly branched and is usually 3–6' tall. However, treelike forms are found that are over 12' in height. The leaves are wedge-shaped with 3 lobes, like big sagebrush, but without the pungent sagebrush aroma. The upper leaf surface is green, while dense hair on the lower surface gives it a gray cast. The leaf margin is rolled under to the lower leaf surface. The yellow flowers are highly fragrant, emitting a strong, pleasant perfume to attract pollinating insects. The flowers have 5 sepals, 5 petals, numerous stamens, and a single pistil.

April–June.

Habitat/Range: Dry slopes of the valleys, foothills, and montane forests.

Comments: Bitterbrush was first described by Frederick Pursh (1774–1820), from a specimen collected by Meriwether Lewis near present-day Ovando, Montana. The label accompanying Lewis' specimen reads: "A shrub common to the open prairie of the knobs, July 6, 1806." Pursh named the species *Tigarea tridentata*, placing it in a genus previously described. His description and detailed illustration of this plant are found in his *Flora Americae Septrentrionalis*, published in 1814 in London. Later, botanists found that the plant did not fit into the genus *Tigarea*, so they created a new genus, naming it in Pursh's honor, *Purshia*. Bitterbrush is a palatable and nutritious browse plant, highly sought after by wild ungulates (deer, elk, etc.) and domestic livestock. Antelope brush is another common name.

Creeping Sibbaldia

CREEPING SIBBALDIA
Sibbaldia procumbens L.
Rose Family (Rosaceae)

Description: This is a ground-hugging plant that forms cushions in the alpine turf. The leaves are compound, with 3 leaflets each, like clover or strawberry leaves. However, creeping sibbaldia leaves are uniquely wedge-shaped, with 3 teeth on the apex. The flowering stems are 1–4" tall, with 2–15 flowers arranged on the end. The tiny flower parts are attached to a shallow, cup-shaped hypanthium. The 5 yellow, spatula-shaped petals are only half the length of the 5 sepals.

June–early August.

Habitat/Range: Moist areas on subalpine ridges and in alpine tundra.

Comments: *Sibbaldia* is named in honor of Sir Robert Sibbald (1641–1722), professor of medicine at Edinburgh. *Procumbens* refers to the prostrate growth form of the plant. Because Sibbaldia is a late snowbank indicator, Scandinavian engineers use it in road design, to point out areas to avoid.

Common Alum Root

COMMON ALUM ROOT
Heuchera parvifolia Nutt.
Saxifrage Family (Saxifragaceae)

Description: The 8–24" tall, slender, and leaf-less stem of common alum root is graced with panicled clusters of tiny greenish white flowers. A close look at the stem with a hand lens will show glandular hairs of various lengths. The stem thrusts out of a dense tuft of basal leaves. The leaves are broadly heart-shaped or kidney-shaped. Rounded or blunt teeth, both deep and shallow, line the leaf margin. The flowers consist of flower parts in fives (sepals, petals, and stamens) attached to a glandular disk that sits on top of the inferior ovary. A hand lens will reveal 2 styles projecting through the center of the disk.

May–September.

Habitat/Range: Variety of conditions from the valleys and foothills to subalpine forest; western MT and WY, central ID.

Comments: *Heuchera* was named in honor of Johann Heinrich von Heucher (1677–1747), a German botanist and physician. It is called alum root because of its alumlike properties. It is valuable as a styptic to stop bleeding and close wounds. The root contains a concentration of tannin, useful medicinally both internally and externally where an astringent is beneficial. It has a long history of medicinal use by Native Americans and folk medicine herbalists, who have used alum root to treat diarrhea, as a poultice for various sores, and to heal ulcers.

SULPHUR PAINTBRUSH
Castilleja sulphurea Rydb.
Figwort Family (Scrophulariaceae)

Description: The colorful leafy bracts of paint-brushes are usually more showy than the flower itself. Sulphur paintbrush has broad, yellow bracts that largely conceal the inconspicuous flowers that can be seen peeking over the top of the bracts. The bracts often have a pair of short, lateral lobes, but these may be absent. The leaves are entire (without lobes) and are shaped like a narrow lance, tapering from the base to the tip. The plants are 8–24" tall.

Late June–September.

Habitat/Range: Subalpine meadows and on open slopes up to timberline.

Comments: Except for the yellow flower color, sulphur paintbrush looks very much like the closely related splitleaf Indian paintbrush (*C. rhexifolia*), which has rose-purple flowers and grows in the same habitat. The yellow western paintbrush (*C. occidentalis*) may be a dwarf alpine form of sulphur paintbrush. They are almost identical, but western paintbrush is 8" or less tall. Western paintbrush is not known from the

Sulphur Paintbrush

Central Rocky Mountains. It is only reported from the Southern Rocky Mountains of Colorado, New Mexico, Utah, and from Glacier National Park in the Northern Rocky Mountains.

YELLOW MONKEY-FLOWER
Mimulus guttatus DC.
Figwort Family (Scrophulariaceae)

Description: The blossoms of yellow monkey-flower often line the edges of streams in the

Yellow Monkey-Flower

Central Rocky Mountains. The plants may grow as annuals or as perennials that spread by creeping stems above the soil surface. They are highly variable in size, sometimes trailing along the ground as low as 2" yet sometimes growing up to 3' tall. The leaves are broad, more or less egg-shaped, and coarsely toothed. The green calyx tube (fused sepals) is ridged and irregularly toothed, with the upper tooth the longest. The yellow corolla tube (fused petals) spreads back into 5 irregular lobes: 2 upper and 3 lower. The flaring throat of the flower is covered with hair and marked with maroon dots on the palate.

March–September.

Habitat/Range: Springs, streams, rivers, ponds, and lakes from moderate to high elevations.

Comments: The name *Mimulus* comes from the Latin *mimus,* likening it to a mimic actor. *Guttatus* is a Latin word meaning "spotted," referring to the small maroon dots on the flower's palate.

Dalmatian Toadflax

DALMATIAN TOADFLAX
Linaria dalmatica (L.) Miller
Figwort Family (Scrophulariaceae)

Description: The showy, snapdragon-like flowers of Dalmatian toadflax thrust upward on spikelike racemes on the ends of 1–3' tall, erect stems. These herbaceous invasive weeds spread by horizontal rootstocks, making control difficult. The leaves are alternate, broadly egg-shaped, have an abrupt, sharp tip, and they clasp the stem at the base. The yellow, tubular flowers are tinged with orange, especially in the hair-lined "mouth." The flower tube flares into 5 lobes: 2 upper lobes and 3 lower lobes. A long, thin spur protrudes from the base of the flower tube.

April–June.

Habitat/Range: Introduced noxious weed; disturbed places, spreading into natural plant communities of the foothills, and montane forests.

Comments: *Linaria* is derived from the Latin *Linum* (flax), because of the vegetative resemblance of the closely related butter-and-eggs (*Linaria vulgaris*) to the common cultivated flax (*Linum usitatissimum*). Like many of our troublesome noxious weeds, dalmatian toadflax came to us from a foreign land, and here lacks the insects and diseases that kept it in balance at home. This gives toadflax a competitive advantage over the native plants in the Central Rocky Mountains, often allowing it to invade and dominate native plant communities. Chemical control has only shown limited success. Ultimately, the introduction of biological control in the form of insects and diseases from its homeland is the only long-term solution. Herbalists view this plant as a phytomedicinal herb, rather than a weed, and use it to treat hepatitis and other liver problems.

Yellow Owl-Clover

YELLOW OWL-CLOVER
Orthocarpus luteus Nutt.
Figwort Family (Scrophulariaceae)

Description: Owl-clovers resemble miniature Indian paintbrushes (*Castilleja* species), to which they are closely related. However, paintbrushes are mostly perennials, and the upper lip of the flower tube is usually much longer than the lower lip. Owl-clovers (*Orthocarpus* species) are all annuals, and both upper and lower lips of the flower tube are of about equal length. Yellow owl-clover has glandular hairs on the sepals and bracts. The bract, below each flower, is divided above the middle into 3 pointed lobes. The leaves are mostly entire, narrow, and pointed, but the upper ones are 3-lobed like the bracts.

July–August.

Habitat/Range: Dry soils from the valleys to montane forests, often in sagebrush communities or open woodlands.

Comments: *Orthocarpus* comes from the Greek *orthos* (straight) and *karpos* (fruit), referring to the straight capsule of owl-clovers. *Luteus* is Latin for "yellow." The botanist Thomas Nuttall (1786–1859) collected the initial specimen of yellow owl-clover, from which the species was first described, "on the plains of the Missouri, near Ft. Mandan," while he traveled with the American Fur Company up the Missouri River in 1811. He described the species in his book *Genera of North American Plants*, published in Philadelphia in 1818.

Bracted Lousewort

BRACTED LOUSEWORT
Pedicularis bracteosa Benth.
Figwort Family (Scrophulariaceae)

Description: Bracted lousewort is sometimes called "fernleaf." The leaves are divided into many long, narrow, toothed segments, like the leaves of many ferns. The leaves are attached well up on the stems, usually without any true basal leaves. The numerous yellow flowers are arranged, spikelike, on the ends of the 1–3' tall, erect, unbranched stems. Each flower arises from the axil of a leafy bract. The flowers are irregular, divided into upper and lower segments. The long upper segment (the galea) is shaped like a hood or helmet on the end. The lower segment has 3 small lobes.

Late June–early August.

Habitat/Range: Moist meadows and open forests in the montane and subalpine forests up to timberline. In the Southern and Central Rocky Mountains the flowers are always yellow. However, red and purple varieties occur in the Northern Rockies and in the Olympic Mountains and Cascades north of Mount Rainier.

Comments: *Bracteosa* refers to the conspicuous leafy bracts below each flower. Louseworts are partially parasitic plants, deriving part of their nutrients from host plants through a root graft. The plant is used by herbalists as a sedative and muscle relaxant.

OEDER'S LOUSEWORT
Pedicularis oederi Vahl
Figwort Family (Scrophulariaceae)

Description: This is a dwarf, alpine lousewort, less than 8" tall. The largest leaves are attached to the base of the plant at or near ground level.

Oeder's Lousewort

On the flowering stem the leaves are few and get progressively smaller up the stem. The individual leaf is divided into many toothed and crowded fernlike segments. A dense, spikelike arrangement of yellow flowers crowns the ends of the short, unbranched stem. The flowers are irregular, divided into upper and lower segments, much like bracted lousewort. The upper segment (the galea) is shaped like a hood and is somewhat shorter than the tube. The crown of the galea is often tinged with purple. The lower segment has 3 small lobes.

July–August.

Habitat/Range: Alpine; Beartooth Mountains of MT and WY.

Comments: Oeder's lousewort was named in honor of George C. Oeder, a Danish botanist. The species was first described in the botanical literature in 1806 from a plant collected in Norway.

WOOLLY MULLEIN
Verbascum thapsus L.
Figwort Family (Scrophulariaceae)

Description: The tall, coarse stalks of woolly mullein stand as allegiant sentinels along the roadsides throughout the long winter. They are biennial plants, growing the first year as a round cluster of radiating basal leaves. The second year, the nutrients stored in the roots are expended in rapid growth of the 1–6' tall or taller flowering stalk. Then, with all its energy expended in reproduction, the plant dies. The basal leaves are unmistakable; they are often as large as 12" long and 4" wide or more and are covered with thick, woolly hair. The leaves on the stem are equally woolly but get progressively smaller up the stem. The stalkless, yellow flowers densely crowd the stem in a tall spike.

June–August.

Habitat/Range: Introduced weed; disturbed places in the valleys, foothills, and montane forests.

Comments: This plant is a scourge to some and an elixir to others. Dioscorides, the Greek physician to the Roman armies in the first century, used mullein to treat coughs, scorpion stings, eye problems, tonsillitis, and toothache. Today,

Woolly Mullein

herbalists value it as a medicinal herb for asthma, bronchitis, coughs, throat inflammation, earache, and various other respiratory complaints. It has also been used as a sedative, a diuretic, and for healing wounds.

Henbane

HENBANE
Hyoscyamus niger L.
Potato Family (Solanaceae)

Description: Henbane is a strongly scented roadside weed. The plants are coarse and very leafy, up to 3' tall, and are covered with fluid-filled, glandular hairs that emit a powerful, tobacco-like odor. The flowers are arranged spikelike, lining up on a single side of the stem. The broadly funnel-shaped petals are greenish yellow with purple veins and throat. The sepals are shaped like an inverted bell, with 5 teeth on the rim. As the ovary matures, the sepals continue to grow, completely enclosing the mature capsule as a hard outer shell. The characteristic 1-sided grouping of hard, bell-like capsules is persistent on the dead plants through the winter.

June–August.

Habitat/Range: Introduced weed; disturbed places in the valleys to the montane forests.

Comments: *Hyoscyamus* comes from the Greek *hys* (sow) and *kyamos* (bean). *Bane* means poison. Henbane was used medicinally for centuries, especially as a pain killer, to induce sleep, and to treat certain nervous system and heart conditions. The witches' brews and ointments of the Middle Ages are known to have included henbane as one of the ingredients for inducing satanic hallucinations. We now know that henbane contains the tropane alkaloids hyoscyamine, scopolamine, and atropine. These substances are highly toxic. The ingestion of even a low dose could be fatal, so keep these plants away from children. They should not be handled or used in any form. Use of henbane in dried flower arrangements may expose children to the toxic seed, and it also eventually scatters the seed to more unwanted places.

Yellow Mountain Violet

YELLOW MOUNTAIN VIOLET
Viola purpurea Kell.
Violet Family (Violaceae)

Description: The pansylike flowers of violets are very familiar and easily recognized. Yellow mountain violet has yellow petals with brown-purple lines. The upper petals are purple on the back. The flowers sometimes fade to a brownish purple color as they age. These are small plants, usually less than 6" tall. They are sometimes called goosefoot violet because of the leaf shape: longer than broad (1½" long and ¾" wide), with a few coarse, shallow lobes ("goose toes"). The leaves are often purplish, at least on the coarse veins.

May–August.

Habitat/Range: Wide variety of conditions from dry to moist; valleys through the high mountains to timberline.

Comments: Violets are nutritious, edible herbs, high in vitamins A and C. They are eaten raw or cooked. A closely related species, yellow prairie violet (*V. nuttallii*), is also common in the Central Rocky Mountains. It is distinguished by having larger leaf blades (greater than 1½" long) that lack the purplish color, lobes, and coarse veins of yellow mountain violet. Also, the upper petals of yellow prairie violet are seldom purple on the back.

GREEN FLOWERS

Green False Hellebore

Pale green to deep green and yellowish green flowers
are included in this section. You may want to check
the white and yellow sections for very pale green or
pale yellowish green flowers if you cannot find
what you are looking for here.

Mountain Maple

MOUNTAIN MAPLE

Acer glabrum Torr.
Maple Family (Aceraceae)

Description: The bright fall foliage is more likely to attract attention to this familiar, tall shrub than are the obscure flowers. Appearing in early spring the short-lived flowers are yellowish green. Each tiny flower is about ⅓" wide and typically has 5 slender sepals, 5 petals, and 8–10 stamens. The pair of broadly winged fruits, joined at the point of attachment, is known as a samara. The opposite leaves are 3-lobed, typical of maples, with an unequally and sharply toothed margin. Sometimes, leaves with 3 separate leaflets are seen. The young twigs are cherry red, turning gray as they age. Mountain maple is a 8–30' tall shrub with graceful, widely spreading branches.

April–June.

Habitat/Range: Moist slopes and along draws and streams from montane to subalpine forests. It is tolerant of shade, often growing under the canopy of conifer trees.

Comments: *Acer* is the Latin name for maple. *Glabrum* means "smooth and without hair." Mountain maple is the most common maple species in the Central Rocky Mountains, although others can be encountered. Box elder (*A. negundo*), with its 3 leaflets, grows along rivers and streams in the foothills and plains. Bigtooth maple (*A. grandidentatum*) is found from near Ashton, Idaho, south through southeastern Idaho and adjacent Wyoming, where its bright orange to red fall color is spectacular. Like its eastern cousins, the western maples can be tapped for making maple syrup.

Raynolds' Sedge

RAYNOLDS' SEDGE
Carex raynoldsii Dewey
Sedge Family (Cyperaceae)

Description: "Sedges have edges" is a rhyme to help us remember that the stems of sedges are triangular in cross section, with the edges felt when rolled between the fingers. In contrast, grasses have round stems (no edges felt when rolled). Raynolds' sedge has sharply edged, triangular stems and grasslike leaves that are 3-ranked when viewed from above. The flower of a sedge is unisexual, consisting of either a pistil or 2–3 stamens, without sepals and petals. Raynolds' sedge has a spike of staminate (male) flowers on the end of the stem, flanked by a few to several spikes of pistillate (female) flowers below. The female flower consists of a black scale and a smooth, green perigynium (a flasklike structure that encloses the pistil). The spikes of the female flowers are therefore 2-toned (green and black). The perigynium is plump, egg-shaped, and not at all flattened. The pistil has 3 styles.

June–August.

Habitat/Range: Moist to dry meadows and open woods from the foothills to the subalpine forests.

Comments: Raynolds' sedge was named in honor of Captain William F. Raynolds, who led the first organized expedition attempting to explore the country now designated as Yellowstone National Park. Although Raynolds' guide was the famous Jim Bridger, he was not successful in penetrating the area from the south as planned. A member of this expedition, Dr. Ferdinand V. Hayden, collected what was to become the type specimen of Raynolds' sedge in Pierre's Hole (the valley of the Snake River in present-day Fremont County, Idaho) on June 20, 1860. Eleven years later, Hayden led the first scientific investigation of the Yellowstone (National Park) country. Raynolds Pass, on the Continental Divide between Idaho and Montana, near Henry's Lake, was on the route of Raynolds' 1860 expedition.

Green-Flowered Wintergreen

GREEN-FLOWERED WINTERGREEN
Pyrola chlorantha Sw.
Heath Family (Ericaceae)

Description: This is a 4–8" tall herbaceous plant of the deep, coniferous forest. The flower petals are pale to yellowish green. The style is curved downward, sticking out beyond the petals on the lower part of the flower. The flowers are arranged in a raceme, with a few (2–8) sparsely spaced flowers distributed on all sides of the flowering stalk. The leaves are pale green on the upper surface and darker green underneath. The usual round shape of the leaves varies somewhat to broadly egg-shaped.

June–August.

Habitat/Range: Moist montane and subalpine forests, often in the shade of coniferous trees.

Comments: *Pyrola* is Latin for "little pear." It is thought to have been given this name because of the pear-shaped leaves of some species. *Chlorantha* is a Greek word meaning "green-flowered." One-sided wintergreen (*P. secunda*) often occurs with green-flowered wintergreen, but it is easily distinguished by its white flowers that are arranged on one side of the flowering stalk. Wintergreen species are medicinal herbs used as a diuretic to treat kidney weakness and chronic kidney infections.

Green Gentian

GREEN GENTIAN
Frasera speciosa Dougl.
Gentian Family (Gentianaceae)

Description: A green gentian leads two lives; a long, modest vegetative phase and a final, dramatic flowering phase. It was once thought to be a biennial, completing its life cycle in two years. However, botanical research has shown that the vegetative phase actually lasts 20–60 years or more. In the vegetative phase the plant grows as a circle of large, radiating basal leaves at ground level. Each leaf is 10–20" long and up to 6" wide. The relative age of the plants can be estimated by comparing the number of leaves per plant: the more leaves, the older the plant. When sufficient food reserves are stored, and the year is right, the plant expends all of its energy in flowering. The climactic flowering stalk is up to 6' tall. Whorls of 3–5 leaves are arranged on this stem in tiers, which get progressively smaller up the stem. The numerous flowers arise at the junctions of these leaves with the stem. Each flower is wheel-shaped, with "spokes" consisting of 4 sepals, 4 petals, and 4 stamens surrounding a prominent superior ovary.

The petals are pale green, flecked with purple, and decorated at the base with a corona of fringe and a pair of hair-lined pits. Once reproduction is complete, the plant dies, leaving the straw-colored skeleton as its own monument. These often protrude through the snow in winter and are still standing the next summer.

June–August.

Habitat/Range: Grasslands, sagebrush slopes, and in open forests from the valleys to the alpine zone.

Comments: The green flowers, broad leaves, and tall, leafy flower stalk of false hellebore (*Veratrum* species) could be mistaken for green gentian. However, false hellebore leaves are pleated, folded like a fan, while green gentian leaves have a smooth surface. False hellebore flowers have 6 petals and 6 stamens, whereas green gentian has flower parts in fours. As a medicinal plant, green gentian is used as a bitter herb to stimulate the digestive system. However, since this plant only flowers once in its long life, collecting it before flowering effectively removes it from the population gene pool. And remember, it may be older than you.

Seaside Arrowgrass

SEASIDE ARROWGRASS
Triglochin maritimum L.
Arrowgrass Family (Juncaginaceae)

Description: Although the narrow leaves of this plant are grasslike, they are thicker and more fleshy than true grass leaves. A close look at the tiny flowers with a hand lens will reveal 6 greenish yellow floral parts and 6 stamens, very unlike the specialized flower parts of grasses. Arrowgrass flowers are rather densely crowded in a long cylindrical arrangement. The flowering stem is 1–3' tall, leafless, and twice the length of the basal leaves. Each flower is attached to the stem with a very short stalk (pedicel), making it appear stalkless. As the fruit dries, it splits open into 6 segments that fall away revealing a round, central axis.

May–August.

Habitat/Range: Marshy areas, wet meadows and especially areas where the soil is high in alkaline minerals, such as saline seeps. In Yellowstone National Park it is often found in the meadows of the geyser basins and hot springs.

Comments: *Triglochin* is named from the Greek *treis* (three) and *glochin* (point), because of the three points on the fruit of some arrow grass species. Seaside arrowgrass is poisonous to livestock, causing death from cyanide poisoning; the plants contain cyanogenetic glycosides, which release hydrocyanic acid when consumed. However, Native Americans are said to have parched the seeds and eaten them. To be safe, young children should be carefully watched when around these plants.

Green False Hellebore

GREEN FALSE HELLEBORE
Veratrum viride Ait.
Lily Family (Liliaceae)

Description: Green false hellebore is a 3–6' tall, herbaceous plant with yellow-green to deep green flowers. The flowers are arranged in open panicles with several branches on the end of the main stem. The lower flower branches droop downward, as if they were wilting. Each small flower has 3 petal-like sepals, 3 petals, and 6 stamens. The distinctive leaves are pleated, with folds like a fan, and are quite large, with the largest leaves 12" long and 6" wide).

June–September.

Habitat/Range: Swamps, streamside shrub thickets, seepy slopes, wet meadows or under the canopy of conifers, especially spruce, from the montane to the subalpine forests. WA, OR, MT, ID. In the Central Rocky Mountains, green false hellebore is replaced by the white-flowered California false hellebore (*V. californicum*) in far southeastern ID, WY.

Comments: *Veratrum* is said to be derived from *vere* (true) and *ater* (black) because of the black rhizomes of some species. The Blackfeet and other Indian tribes were known to dig these rhizomes as a medicinal herb called "makes-you-sneeze-root." The shavings from the dry root were sniffed up the nose to relieve nasal congestion. Other Native Americans used the plant as a permanent contraceptive and to treat snakebites. In Western medicine these practices seem very hazardous, considering the high toxicity of these plants. *Veratrum* is known to contain compounds with a variety of physiological effects. They are especially potent as a heart depressant, in lowering blood pressure, and inducing congenital malformation in the fetus. Pregnant ewes feeding on false hellebore often bear "monkey-face" lambs, a fatal deformity. Other compounds in the plant have been shown to have value as an insecticide. False hellebore is a dangerous, poisonous plant with potentially fatal results if ingested.

Early Coralroot

EARLY CORALROOT
Corallorhiza trifida Chatel
Orchid Family (Orchidaceae)

Description: In the deep shade of the forest floor, clusters of bright chartreuse stems often call attention to this small orchid. The plant is leafless, but it has 2 or 3 tubular bracts that sheath the stem. The stems and bracts are yellowish green. The plant bears 3–15 flowers. The flowers have a white lip, sometimes with a few purple spots. The sepals and petals range from yellow to green and thrust forward past the lip. These small plants are 2–10" tall and flowering is short-lived.

June–early August.

Habitat/Range: Montane and subalpine forest floors rich with organic matter, often in deep shade.

Comments: Coralroots derive nutrients and energy from the rotting organic matter on the forest floor. This the coralroot accomplishes by parasitizing fungi inhabiting its root system that in turn parasitize trees and digest wood. The recycled wood is thus put to good use supporting these lovely plants. Early coralroot also has some chlorophyll in all of its plant parts, enabling it to capture the sun's energy through photosynthesis and supplement that derived from the fungi.

Small Northern Bog Orchid

SMALL NORTHERN BOG ORCHID

Habenaria obtusata (Banks ex Pursh) Rich.
(Also *Platanthera obtusata* (Banks ex Pursh) Lind.)
Orchid Family (Orchidaceae)

Description: The solitary leaf and small greenish white flowers of this bog orchid make it easy to distinguish from others in the Central Rocky Mountains. The single leaf is oblong, blunt on the end, and gradually tapers toward the sheathing base. The stem is about 3-12" tall and bears 3-15 widely spaced flowers. The flowers have a long-tapering, strap-shaped lip petal, slightly upturned at the tip. The spur is also long-tapering and about equal to the blade of the lip petal in length.

June–July.

Habitat/Range: Wet forests, often under spruce trees, and in marshes, bogs, and along stream banks; eastern WA, northern ID, MT, WY, and the Wallowa Mountains of OR.

Comments: *Platanthera* comes from the Greek *platys* (wide) and *anthera* (anther) because of the unusually wide anthers in these plants. Bog orchids are included in the genus *Habenaria* or *Platanthera,* depending on the floral manual consulted. Small northern bog orchid is pollinated by mosquitoes, which are abundant in their habitat.

Northern Twayblade

NORTHERN TWAYBLADE
Listera borealis Morong
Orchid Family (Orchidaceae)

Description: Northern twayblade has a pair of opposite leaves above the middle of the stem and a raceme of 3–15 tiny green flowers on the end. The entire plant grows up to 10" tall. The leaves are dark bluish green and as large as 2" long and 1" wide. The flower has an odd, strap-shaped "lip" petal with 2 lobes and is covered with minutely short hair. The other small sepals and petals are swept back away from the lip, like ears. A curved column rises like a horn at the base from the lip, where the sepals and petals join. The flower reminds me of a strange, one-horned, green cow that must belong to some forest leprechaun.

June–July.

Habitat/Range: Old-growth, moist, and mossy forests of the subalpine zone; north-central WA, ID, western MT, western WY.

Comments: *Listera* was named in honor of an English physician, Martin Lister (1638–1711). *Borealis* refers to its boreal (northern) habitat range. Orchids are highly evolved plants that have developed specialized and complex reproductive systems. Twayblades have an unusual mechanism for insuring cross-pollination. A trail of nectar on the lip attracts small insects and leads them to the base of the column. Movement of the insect there triggers the plant to forcefully eject a droplet of liquid glue onto the insect, and some pollen becomes firmly fixed to the droplet. Frightened by this action, the insect flies away to another flower, where the pollen is then deposited on the stigma at the base of the column.

Mountain Sorrel

MOUNTAIN SORREL
Oxyria digyna (L.) Hill
Buckwheat Family (Polygonaceae)

Description: The abundant kidney-shaped basal leaves of this plant are distinctive. The leaf texture is tender and succulent. A leafy sheath (stipule) encloses the stem at the attachment of the leaf petiole. The stems are 4–16" tall, crowded with numerous flowers and fruit. The flowers are green, tinged with red, and consist of 4 floral segments (2 narrow, 2 broad), 6 stamens, and an ovary with a curious, fringed stigma. The floral segments are tiny when in bloom, but they expand as the fertilized ovary rapidly grows into a flattened and winged fruit about ¼" long.

July–August.

Habitat/Range: Scant soil between talus boulders and rock crevices on subalpine and alpine ridges.

Comments: *Oxyria* comes from the Greek *oxys,* meaning "sharp." The juice of mountain sorrel is sharply acidic, like lemon juice. The foliage is edible, and a taste of the leaves is a refreshing treat. However, the oxalic acid, which is responsible for the sharp taste, is known to change to a precipitate of calcium oxalate in the bloodstream, where it tends to impede kidney function. Many other plants in the buckwheat family share this charactcristic, including garden spinach. Cultivated rhubarb has a highly poisonous concentration of oxalic acid in its leaf tissue. In 1919, a medical journal recorded the death of a Montana woman thirty-six hours after eating a meal of fried rhubarb leaves.

Western Meadow-Rue (male)

Western Meadow-Rue (female)

WESTERN MEADOW-RUE
Thalictrum occidentale A. Gray
Buttercup Family (Ranunculaceae)

Description: At first glance, western meadow-rue leaves look just like columbine leaves (*Aquilegia* species). However, columbines in the Central Rocky Mountains have leaves that are twice ternate (3 x 3), with a total of 9 leaflets per compound leaf. Western meadow-rue leaves are at least 3 times ternate (3 x 3 x 3), with a total of 27 leaflets (or more) per leaf. In addition, most of the leaves of our columbines originate from the plant base, with only a few reduced leaves on the flowering stem. Western meadow-rue has most of its leaves up on the main stems, with seldom any from the base. Meadow-rue lacks the colorful, showy flowers of columbine. Instead, it has rather inconspicuous unisexual flowers (and plants), with the female and male flowers occurring on separate plants. The flowers lack petals, consisting only of the greenish sepals, tinged with purple, and either pistils or stamens. The male flowers look like wind chimes, the anthers quivering with the slightest breeze on the ends of the delicate, flexible filaments.

May–August.

Habitat/Range: Cool, moist woods, from the montane to subalpine forest.

Comments: Native Americans have used this plant variously as a medicine in treating headaches, nasal congestion, and other complaints; as a love charm in seeking the affection of a lover; and as a stimulant to horses, placed in their nostrils to increase endurance. Meadow-rue is among the plants being investigated for naturally occurring bioagents in cancer chemotherapy research.

Tweedy's Willow

TWEEDY'S WILLOW
Salix tweedyi (Beeb) Ball
Willow Family (Salicaceae)

Description: Almost everyone recognizes willows as a group and knows the "pussy willow" flower clusters (catkins) that they bear. Distinguishing individual species of willow requires careful attention to detail (and a hand lens). Willow flowers are tiny and unisexual, with male and female flowers on separate plants. An individual flower consists simply of 2 stamens (male) or a pistil (female). Attached to the base of each flower is a scalelike bract, often covered with hair. Tweedy's willow has scales that are distinctly black and covered with dense, long hair. The pistil of its female flower is smooth (hairless) and has an unusually long style (up to ⅛" or more). The catkins are attached directly to the twigs, often from the end of the previous year's twig growth. The leaves are broad, equally dark green on both surfaces, and thinly clad with long hairs. This is a tall shrub, up to 9' or more, with hairy and unusually stout twigs. The "pussy willow" catkins often appear before the leaves, or just as they are breaking bud.

June–early July.

Habitat/Range: Stream banks, lakeshores, and wet meadows in subalpine forests; northeastern WA, central and northern ID, western MT, and western and central WY (especially the Bighorn Mountains).

Comments: *Salix* is said to be derived from the Celtic words *sal* (near) and *lis* (water), because it is frequently found near water. Tweedy's willow is named in honor of Frank Tweedy (1854–1937), who collected the type specimen at the head of Big Goose Creek in the Bighorn Mountains of Wyoming in 1896. Willows have a long history of medicinal use from the time of the Greek physician Dioscordes in the first century A.D., if not earlier. North American Indians also used willow to relieve pain and other complaints. The bark contains salicin, which changes to salicylic acid when ingested. Salicylic acid is effective in treating skin diseases and in bringing relief for headaches, neuralgia, and arthritis. In 1899, the Bayer Company synthesized aspirin in the laboratory as a substitute for salicylic acid, with the side effect of stomach irritation much reduced.

Bog Saxifrage

BOG SAXIFRAGE
Saxifraga oregana Howell
Saxifrage Family (Saxifragaceae)

Description: Bog saxifrage is 1–2' tall, with 2–7" long leaves that originate from the base. The leaves are usually widest above the middle and taper gradually to the base. The stems are leafless, often purple, and covered with fine, gland-tipped hairs. About 100 flowers are arranged in small clusters on the stems. Each tiny flower has 5 sepals, up to 5 petals, 10 stamens, and a pistil parted into 2 segments above the middle. The petals are greenish white when present, but are more often missing.

May–August.

Habitat/Range: Wet meadows, often below persistent snowbanks or along streams; western WA, OR, ID, western MT, and WY.

Comments: The name *Saxifraga* comes from the Latin *saxum* (rock) and *frango* (to break). According to the doctrine of signatures, early herbalists believed that the granular bulblets found in certain species of these plants indicated that the herb would dissolve urinary stones.

Common Cattail

COMMON CATTAIL
Typha latifolia L.
Cattail Family (Typhaceae)

Description: The long, flat, straplike leaves and the cylindrical, dense flower masses of cattails are familiar to all. Cattails have unisexual flowers, with the top ⅓–½ of the "cattail" consisting of pollen-bearing male flowers. The bottom portion of the cylindrical flower mass consists of the tightly packed pistillate flowers, which are green when young and fresh but turn dark brown as the stigmas dry and the plant matures. In the common cattail the male and female segments are normally contiguous. Lesser cattail (*T. angustifolia*) is a related species, with the male and female segments separated by a gap on the naked flower stalk ½–2" wide. The long, flat leaves of common cattail are ⅜–1" wide, while lesser cattail has narrower leaves, less than ⅜" in width.

June–August.

Habitat/Range: Shallow, slow-moving water along marshy places, streams, and lakes from the plains and valleys to the montane forests.

Comments: Every part of the cattail plant was important to the Native Americans. The pollen of cattail was sacred to some tribes. The flowering of cattail was said to announce the maturing of corn. The pollen, the young flower spikes, and the long rhizomes were eaten. The leaves were woven into mats. On November 21, 1805, near the mouth of the Columbia River, the explorer William Clark recorded in his journals: "we also purchased hats made of Grass &c. of those Indians, Some very handsom mats made of flags" (flag is another common name for cattail). The down from cattails has had a variety of uses: as a dressing for treating burns, as a filling for pillows, as padding for cradle boards, and as a diaperlike absorbent padding for infants' bottoms.

Nettle

NETTLE
Urtica dioica L.
Nettle Family (Urticaceae)

Description: Unfortunately, this plant is more often identified accidentally by touch (ouch!) than by sight. The leaves and stems are covered with stinging hairs that contain histamine-like substances. Contact with the skin can cause a sharp burning pain and an acute allergic dermatitis. In favorable locations nettles can grow to 9' tall, although they are more often closer to 3' tall in the Central Rocky Mountains. The plants have opposite, toothed leaves and flowers in the leaf axils, similar to plants in the mint family. However, unlike mints, nettles have inconspicuous, green, unisexual flowers. Within North America, the male and female flowers usually occur on the same (monoecious) plant.

June–September.

Habitat/Range: Streams in the valleys, but it also grows on moist, seepy mountain slopes; sea level to the subalpine forests.

Comments: *Urtica* comes from *uro* (to burn), an appropriate name considering the sharp, burning sensation on the skin when the plant is touched. Surprisingly, the plant is considered an important edible and medicinal plant, rendered harmless by cooking. Nettle greens are rich in minerals, vitamins, and protein. An old European folk remedy for arthritis and rheumatism consisted of flailing the affected body parts with nettle stems, a practice known as "urtication." Modern herbalists value the plant for its astringent and diuretic properties, especially for treating internal bleeding or water retention.

Lodgepole Pine Dwarf Mistletoe

LODGEPOLE PINE DWARF MISTLETOE

Arceuthobium americanum Nutt.
Mistletoe Family (Viscaceae)

Description: It takes a keen observer to notice these small parasitic shrubs growing out of the branches of lodgepole pine trees. The delicate, branching stems are seldom over 2" long, or about the length of the needles of the pine tree. There are no broad leaves as there are on Christmas mistletoe, only pairs of opposite scales, joined at the base. The unisexual flowers are equally obscure, consisting of 2–4 greenish floral lobes and either anthers or pistils. The male flowers, with the anthers, have a single anther attached directly to the inner surface of each floral lobe. The floral lobes of the female, pistillate, flower are attached to the ovary. The ovary requires a full year to progress from flowering to mature fruit.

April–July

Habitat/Range: This species of dwarf mistletoe is parasitic on pine trees only, mostly on lodgepole pine (*Pinus contorta*). It is occasionally found on whitebark pine (*Pinus albicaulis*) in the Central Rocky Mountains.

Comments: *Arceuthobium* comes from the Greek word *arkeuthos,* meaning "juniper," and *bios,* meaning "life." Dwarf mistletoe species are parasitic on juniper as well as many other conifers. As the ovary of dwarf mistletoe matures, pressure builds up in the tissues until it explodes, forcefully ejecting the seed across distances of 30' or more. The seed has a sticky coating, which adheres to whatever it comes into contact with. If it sticks to the bark of a host conifer, it will germinate and penetrate the bark. Here the dwarf mistletoe plant establishes its parasitic relationship, with its "root system" in the inner bark, or cambium, drawing nutrients from the tissues of the host tree as needed. The response of the host tree is to form swellings on the infected stems and abnormal, dense masses of stems called witches'-brooms.

WHITE FLOWERS

White Mule's-Ears

This section is for pure white flowers, although many white flowers vary from white to very pale green or very pale yellow. Other white flowers fade to pink or lavender or some other color as they age. If you cannot find the flowers you are looking for here, you may want to check the green and yellow sections.

Arrowhead

ARROWHEAD
Sagittaria cuneata Sheld.
Water-Plantain Family (Alismataceae)

Description: Arrowhead has distinctive leaves, shaped just like an arrowhead. This is an aquatic plant, rooted in the mud; the leaves originate from the plant base, often underwater, and emerge above the water's surface. The flowers occur in groups of 3 along the leafless stem. Each flower has 3 greenish sepals and 3 white petals. The flowers are unisexual, with female (seed-bearing) flowers on the lower portion of each stem, and the male (pollen-producing) flowers on the upper stem.

June–September.

Habitat/Range: Ponds, streams, and swamps.

Comments: The arrowhead was known as *wapato* by Native Americans of western Washington and Oregon and was a major food source for them. On March 29, 1806, soon after starting the return journey up the Columbia River from Fort Clatsop, Meriwether Lewis noted in his journal, "the wappetoe furnishes the principal article of traffic with these people . . . the natives of the Sea coast . . . will dispose of their most valuable articles to obtain this root"; and William Clark wrote, "they Collect great quantities of pappato, which the womin collect by getting into the water, Sometimes to their necks holding by a Small canoe and with their feet loosen the wappato or bulb of the root from the bottom from the fibers, and it imedeately rises to the top of the water, they Collect & throw them into the Canoe."

Lyall's Angelica

LYALL'S ANGELICA
Angelica arguta Nutt.
Parsley Family (Apiaceae)

Description: Lyall's angelica is a large, perennial herbaceous plant 1–6' tall. The leaves are twice compound, with 11–23 leaflets per leaf. Teeth line the margin of the leaflets. Each leaflet is rather large, usually 2–5" long. The lateral leaf veins are directed to the end of the tooth on the leaf margin, rather than the notch between the teeth. The numerous white (or pinkish) flowers are densely arranged in the compound umbels. The fruit is flattened dorsally, that is, on the back, parallel to the joint between the 2 segments. The ribs on the margin and the back of the fruit are elongated into obvious "wings," with the marginal wings much broader than the ones on the back. The fruit is smooth (hairless).

June–August.

Habitat/Range: Stream sides, lakeshores, and wet meadows in the montane and subalpine forests.

Comments: *Angelica* is named from the Latin *angelus* or angel, because of the beneficial qualities of the herb. *Arguta* means "sharp-toothed," descriptive of the sharp teeth on the leaf margin. This species is named for David Lyall, a British botanist and geologist who collected the plant while working on the boundary survey between Canada and the western United States in the 1880s. *Angelica* species have long been prized by herbalists for improving digestion, reducing gas, and loosening phlegm in bronchitis. They also promote sweating and urination for eliminating toxins. Unfortunately, *Angelica* is so similar in both appearance and habitat to water hemlock (*Cicuta* species), the most toxic plants in North America, that it is too dangerous to risk misidentification.

Water Hemlock

WATER HEMLOCK
Cicuta maculata L.
(Also *C. douglasii* (DC.) Coult. and Rose)
Parsley Family (Apiaceae)

Description: The primary lateral veins of the leaf of water hemlock are most often directed to the notch between the teeth, best seen by holding a leaflet up to the light. This venation is unique, separating water hemlock from other parsley family plants in the Rocky Mountains. The fruit is round or broadly oval, with ribs that are nearly equal in size and not expanded or winged.

Habitat/Range: Stream sides, wet meadows, and other marshy places in the plains and valleys usually below 7,000 feet in elevation.

Comments: Water hemlock has the reputation of being the most violently poisonous plant in the north temperate zone. Many human and livestock fatalities have resulted from ingesting even small portions of the plant, especially the root. The poisonous compound in water hemlock, cicutoxin, acts on the central nervous system causing violent convulsions, interspersed with periods of relaxation. Death usually occurs from 15 minutes to 8 hours after ingesting a lethal dose. Accidental poisonings happen most frequently because water hemlock is mistaken for edible members of the parsley family, which it resembles in both appearance and odor. One should never experiment with eating wild food plants without verifying the plant identification with an expert.

Poison Hemlock

POISON HEMLOCK
Conium maculatum L.
Parsley Family (Apiaceae)

Description: Poison hemlock often grows 4–9' tall, with leaves that are finely dissected into numerous small segments, like carrot or parsley leaves. Its purple-spotted stems are the key distinguishing characteristic. It is a biennial, growing as a low, leafy plant the first year. The second growing season the plant rapidly shoots upward on tall flowering stems. The white flowers are arranged in compound umbels on the end of the stems and the leaf axils. The fruit is round or broadly oval, with ribs that are nearly equal in size and somewhat wavy. The plants die at the end of the season in which they flower and fruit, leaving tall, straw-colored stalks that often persist throughout the winter.

May–September.

Habitat/Range: Introduced weed; disturbed areas.

Comments: This is the hemlock that was used to put Socrates to death in 399 B.C. Symptoms of poisoning appear as soon as twelve minutes after ingestion. At first it acts as a stimulant, causing nervousness and trembling. This is soon followed by slowed heartbeat, paralysis and coldness of the legs and arms, and finally death by respiratory failure. In Africa the poison has been used on darts and arrows. Poisoning of humans often occurs because of the resemblance of the foliage to parsley, or the seeds to anise or caraway. Sampling of wild food plants is a dangerous, potentially lethal activity.

HAYDEN'S CYMOPTERUS
Cymopterus bipinnatus Wats.
(Also *C. nivalis* Wats.)
Parsley Family (Apiaceae)

Description: The leaves are blue-green and compound, finely divided into many small, narrow segments. Old leaf stalks from several previous years are persistent on the woody base below the new leaves. The leafless stems are 2–10" tall, each with several clusters of white flowers arranged in compound umbels on the end. The fruit is broadly oval-oblong, with winged ribs of about equal size.

May–July.

Habitat/Range: Rocky outcrops and slopes; foothills and montane forests to the alpine.

Hayden's Cymopterus

Comments: It is called Hayden's cymopterus in honor of Dr. Ferdinand V. Hayden, a naturalist and early explorer. Hayden was a member of the first organized party to attempt the exploration of present-day Yellowstone National Park in 1860. Then, in 1871–1872, as head of the U.S. Geological Survey, Dr. Hayden organized and led a large survey party in conducting the first scientific exploration of the Yellowstone and Grand Teton areas. Hayden collected this species of *Cymopterus* in the Central Rocky Mountains south of Virginia City, Montana.

COW PARSNIP
Heracleum lanatum Michx.
Parsley Family (Apiaceae)

Cow Parsnip

Description: Cow parsnip leaves consists of 3 large leaflets that are 4–12" long and equally wide. The leaflets are palmately lobed and have a double-toothed margin. The plant is 3–6' tall and covered with long, silky, straight hairs. Cow parsnip's umbels of white flowers are often quite large. The terminal one is as much as 8" across and the rays as much as 4" long. The fruit is strongly flattened laterally, that is, on the back and parallel to the joint between the fruit segments. The veins on the back of the fruit are not expanded into wings, but the lateral, marginal veins are.

June–August.

Habitat/Range: Moist, low places in the valley, montane forests, and lower subalpine forests.

Comments: These plants are rich in minerals and relished by grazing animals, hence the name cow parsnip. In herbal medicine the plants were long used to treat epilepsy. Cow parsnip is known to contain compounds that cause photodermatitis in humans, a toxic reaction causing a sunburnlike rash when one is exposed to both the plant and ultraviolet radiation.

Fern-Leaved Lovage

FERN-LEAVED LOVAGE
Ligusticum filicinum Wats.
Parsley Family (Apiaceae)

Description: Fern-leaved lovage has very finely dissected leaves, somewhat like poison hemlock, but without the purple spots on the stems. It is also smaller than poison hemlock, usually 2–4' tall. Vegetatively it is more likely confused with fern-leaved desert parsley (*Lomatium dissectum*). However, the fruit of lovage is oblong, almost round in cross section, with narrowly winged ribs on the back. Desert parsley has fruit that is strongly flattened, without winged ribs on the back, but with a strongly winged margin. The white flowers of lovage are arranged in compound umbels.

June–August.

Habitat/Range: Meadows or open woods in the montane and subalpine forests near timberline; eastern ID, western WY, and southwestern MT.

Comments: *Ligusticum* is named for the Italian province of Liguria. At least four species of *Ligusticum* occur in the Central Rocky Mountains. Species of *Ligusticum* are found in Chinese medicine, including *chuan xiong* (*L. wallichii*), which is used as a sedative and for reducing blood pressure. Osha (*L. porteri*) is widely used in herbal folk medicine in the Southern Rocky Mountains of Colorado and New Mexico for treating sore throats associated with the common cold and other viral infections.

Yampah

YAMPAH
Perideridia montana (Blank) Dorn
(Also *Perideridia gairdneri* (H. & A.) Math.)
Parsley Family (Apiaceae)

Description: The leaves of yampah are compound with 3–5 long, narrow, linear segments. The leaves begin to wilt and dry up as the flowers fade and the fruit appears. The white flowers are arranged in compound umbels on top of slender stems 1–4' tall. The fruit is round and scarcely (if at all) flattened. Yampah looks very similar to bulb-bearing water hemlock (*Cicuta bulbifera*), a highly poisonous plant. However, *Cicuta bulbifera* has tiny bulbs in the axils of some of the upper leaves, and it usually grows adjacent to water or on marshy ground.

July–August.

Habitat/Range: Meadows and open forests from the valleys to the subalpine forests.

Comments: Yampah was among the most important food plants of the Native Americans within its range. On August 26, 1805, while among the Shoshone Indians near present-day Lemhi Pass in Idaho and Montana, Meriwether Lewis wrote in his journal: "I observe the indian women collecting the root of a species of fennel which grows in the moist grounds and feeding their poor starved children; (the root) is white firm and crisp in its present state, when dried and pounded it makes a fine white meal." A detailed, clear botanical description of the yampah is included in this portion of the journal. Because of the similarity to poisonous bulb-bearing water hemlock, extreme caution is advised.

YARROW
Achillea millefolium L.
Aster Family (Asteraceae)

Description: This common plant is easily recognized by its fine, lacy, fernlike leaves and

Yarrow

its distinctive aroma. It is a perennial, herbaceous plant 8–24" tall. The leaves are evenly distributed along the stem, but the largest leaves are on the lower portion, and they get progressively smaller up the stem. The numerous flower heads are in a flattopped arrangement on the end of the stems. The flower petals are normally white (rarely pink).

April–October.

Habitat/Range: Variety of conditions, seaside to the alpine summits.

Comments: *Achillea* is named for Achilles, the Greek warrior and hero of Homer's *Iliad*. It is supposed to have been used to treat the wounds of soldiers during the Trojan War. *Millefolium* means "a thousand leaves"—very descriptive of yarrow leaves, which are finely dissected into perhaps a thousand segments. Yarrow has been used for medicinal purposes throughout history. It is especially useful in stopping bleeding by encouraging blood clotting. The herb has also been used to promote urination and sweating, as a digestive aid, for treating colds and flu, and to alleviate menstrual disorders.

PEARLY EVERLASTING
Anaphalis margaritacea (L.) Benth. & Hook.
Aster Family (Asteraceae)

Description: This plant is often confused with pussytoes (*Antennaria*), which it closely resembles. However, pussytoes has well-developed basal leaves, while those on the stems get progressively smaller upward. Pearly everlasting lacks basal leaves. Instead, it has leaves of about the same size equally distributed along the stems. By the time of flowering, the lower leaves on the stem have withered. The underside of the leaf of pearly everlasting is covered with dense, white hair. The top of the leaf is green and smooth or only thinly hairy. It is an upright plant, with stems 8–36" tall. The heads have tiny, inconspicuous disk flowers, without showy rays around the margin. The bracts around the margin of the flower heads are pearly white, sometimes with a small dark spot at the base.

July–October.

Habitat/Range: Disturbed places and forest openings in the montane and subalpine forests.

Pearly Everlasting

Comments: The persistent white bracts that surround the numerous flower heads make excellent dry floral arrangements, hence the name pearly everlasting.

TALL PUSSYTOES
Antennaria anaphaloides Rydb.
Aster Family (Asteraceae)

Description: This is a large (for pussytoes), upright plant, 8–20" tall, resembling pearly everlasting. However, tall pussytoes is distinguished by its large, well-developed basal leaves and the smaller stem leaves that are reduced in size progressively upward on the stem. The surfaces of the leaves are equally woolly-hairy on both sides. The flower heads consist of tiny disk flowers only, with no showy rays. The bracts around the margin of the heads are white, thin, and translucent, often with a basal dark spot.

June–August.

Habitat/Range: Foothills and montane forests.

Comments: *Antennaria* is named for the resemblance of the modified sepals (pappus) of the male flowers to the antennae of a small insect. Native American people used pussytoes for various medicinal purposes ranging from rattlesnake bites to coughs.

Tall Pussytoes

ROSY PUSSYTOES
Antennaria microphylla Rydb.
Aster Family (Asteraceae)

Rosy Pussytoes

Description: Rosy pussytoes is a low, mat-forming perennial that spreads by trailing stems. The leaves are gray, equally woolly-hairy on both surfaces, and spatula-shaped. The basal leaves are larger than the sparse leaves on the slender stem. Surrounding the flower heads are several series of overlapping bracts, which are dry, thin, and translucent. The color of the bracts varies from white to rosy red. They lack the basal dark spot of tall pussytoes.

June–August.

Habitat/Range: Valleys to the lower subalpine forests.

Comments: *Microphylla* refers to the bracts (phyllaries) that surround the flower heads, which are smaller in rosy pussytoes than in most other species of *Antennaria*. According to herbalists, pussytoes is a mild astringent herb, useful in quieting simple intestinal and liver inflammations.

Silver Sagebrush

SILVER SAGEBRUSH
Artemisia cana Pursh
Aster Family (Asteraceae)

Description: The silvery foliage and pungent aroma of sagebrush is familiar in the western United States where it is often the dominant vegetation. Silver sagebrush is distinguished by its leaves, which are mostly entire (without teeth), long, and linear. Occasionally a few leaves are found with 1–3 teeth on the end of the leaf. Big sagebrush (*A. tridentata*), and all of the other woody sagebrush species in the Central Rocky Mountains, have leaves that are all 3-toothed or more deeply divided into 3–5 segments. Silver sagebrush is usually 2–4' tall and spreads by underground stems.

August–October.

Habitat/Range: Meadows in the valleys, sagebrush steppes, foothills, and montane forests, especially in swales and coulee bottoms with heavy soils and slower drainage.

Comments: *Artemisia* was named for Artemis, the goddess of the moon, wild animals, and hunting in Greek mythology. *Cana* refers to the silvery-gray hair which gives the plant its silvery sheen. Silver sagebrush is well adapted to the wildfires that have swept its habitat for thousands of years. When burned to the ground it simply resprouts from surviving buds on horizontal stems below the soil surface. In contrast, big sagebrush is more often killed by fire, so it must rely on its seed to recolonize the burned area. Silver sagebrush was first described to botanical science by Frederick Pursh in 1814, from an October 1804 collection made by Meriwether Lewis near the mouth of the Cheyenne River, in present-day South Dakota.

ENGELMANN'S ASTER
Aster engelmannii (Eat.) Gray
Aster Family (Asteraceae)

Description: A close look at a flower head shows that it consists of 8–13 showy white (or pale pink) ray flowers surrounding the numerous golden yellow disk flowers. The bracts around the base of the flower head overlap like roof shingles. Each bract has a strong midvein and is often keeled like the bottom of a boat. The plants are rather large, often 2–4' tall or taller. The leaves midway on the stem are the largest, while the lowest leaves are much smaller and sometimes even scalelike. The leaves are lance-shaped and average about 3" in length and 1" in width.

July–September.

Habitat/Range: Moist montane and subalpine forests.

Comments: Engelmann's aster is named in honor of the famous St. Louis botanist, physician, and meteorologist, George Engelmann (1809–1884). In the mid-1840s, he and the

Engelmann's Aster

Harvard botanist Asa Gray promoted western plant collection by providing equipment and instruction to explorers and analyzing the specimens they brought back.

BLUE-LEAVED ASTER
Aster glaucodes Blake
Aster Family (Asteraceae)

Description: Like Engelmann's aster, this species has white (or pale lavender) ray flowers,

Blue-Leaved Aster

keeled bracts, and lower stem leaves that are small or even scalelike. However, blue-leaved aster is a smaller plant (1–2' tall), with a glaucous coating on the leaves (a whitish substance that rubs off). The leaves are about as long as those of Engelmann's aster, but narrower and more oblong. The ray flowers surround a bright yellow disk.

July–September.

Habitat/Range: Rocky, dry places in the montane and subalpine forests; northwestern WY, southeastern ID.

Comments: This species and several other asters (at least 6) are known to accumulate selenium in their tissues, often to toxic levels. They are said to be facultative (or secondary) selenium absorbers. This means that although they do not require the element for proper growth, they nevertheless absorb it to high levels when it is present in the soil. Many species of milkvetch (*Astragalus*) also accumulate selenium, some requiring it for proper growth. Selenium poisoning of livestock is a serious problem in western North America.

Tasselflower

TASSELFLOWER
Brickellia grandiflora (Hook.) Nutt.
Aster Family (Asteraceae)

Description: The nodding flower heads of tasselflower look like the tassels on graduation caps, except the "fringe" is short. The heads appear heavy for their slender stalks (peduncles), and they swing freely in the breeze. There are fine, parallel lines (striations) lengthwise on the flower bracts around the base of the flower head. The outer, or lowest, bracts are tipped with a slender tentacle. The heads include only disk flowers, without showy rays. The petals are creamy white to buff or pale yellowish. The triangular to arrowhead-shaped leaves are about 4" or less in length and are very distinctive. The lowest leaves on the stems soon fall off, leaving only the middle to upper leaves by the time of flowering.

July–October.

Habitat/Range: Dry, rocky soil in the montane and subalpine forests.

Comments: *Brickellia* was named in honor of John Brickell (1749–1809) who was a physician and botanist in Savannah, Georgia.

CUT-LEAVED DAISY
Erigeron compositus Pursh
Aster Family (Asteraceae)

Description: The basal leaves of this daisy consist of many narrow, branching segments, with 1–4 groups of 3 leaflets each. The few leaves on the stems are small and often unbranched. The stem seldom exceeds 10" in height, and has a single flower head. The flower head usually consists of white rays surrounding a yellow disk. Sometimes the rays are pink or blue, but occasionally there are no ray flowers at all. The bracts around the base of the flower head are in a single row, and they have glands and spreading hairs.

May–August.

Habitat/Range: Thin, poorly developed soil.

Comments: *Compositus* is a Latin word meaning "compound," of many parts, referring to the compound, many-divided leaves of cut-leaved daisy. The leaves are the distinguishing feature

Cut-Leaved Daisy

of this species. In 1806 Meriwether Lewis collected a specimen of cut-leaved daisy near present day Kamiah, Idaho, while the Lewis and Clark Expedition was waiting for the snow to sufficiently melt for safe passage over Lolo Pass.

Elk Thistle

ELK THISTLE
Cirsium scariosum Nutt.
Aster Family (Asteraceae)

Description: The leaf base of elk thistle clasps the stem and does not extend ridgelike down the stem, as it does in Tweedy's thistle (*C. tweedyi*) and several others. The leafy bracts around the base of each flower head lack the glandular ridge of wavy-leaved thistle (*C. undulatum*) and certain other species. The tip of the inner bracts of elk thistle is dilated, with a margin that is scarious (thin, parchmentlike) and fringed. Elk thistle is a stout plant, up to 3' (or even 6') tall, with thick, fleshy stems that taper little from the base to the top. The flower color varies from white to somewhat yellowish, tan, pink, or lavender. The flower heads are densely clustered on and adjacent to the top of the thick stem. This is a biennial species, growing as a cluster of radiating basal leaves the first year (or perhaps more). The second (or subsequent) year the plant sends up the large flowering stem, flowers, and then dies.

June–August.

Habitat/Range: Moist mountain meadows.

Comments: Elk thistle is often called Everts' thistle in Yellowstone National Park. This name honors Truman Everts, a member of the Washburn Expedition that explored what is now Yellowstone National Park in 1870. Everts became separated from the Washburn party and lost his horse and all belongings except for a small knife and opera glass. Enduring snowstorms and the lack of any means to secure better food, Everts subsisted almost exclusively on thistle roots for nearly a month, until rescued (near death at about 50 pounds) by John Baronett on October 6. This plant and a mountain in Yellowstone National Park are named for Evert, while Yellowstone's Baronett Peak honors his rescuer.

ARROW-LEAVED COLTSFOOT
Petasites sagittatus (Banks) Gray
Aster Family (Asteraceae)

Description: Arrow-leaved coltsfoot has flower heads with whitish disk flowers that bloom

Arrow-Leaved Coltsfoot

before the leaves emerge. Later the large, arrowhead-shaped basal leaves develop to a length of up to 12". White, woolly hair covers the underside of the leaves. Instead of true leaves on the stem, it has a series of overlapping bracts, with parallel veins.

April–June.

Habitat/Range: Wetlands of the montane and subalpine forests.

Comments: *Petasites* is derived from the Greek word *petasos,* a type of "broad-brimmed hat," probably because of the large leaves of this plant. Species of *Petasites* have long been used in both European and American herbal medicine for treating coughs, asthma, and intestinal colic. It is also a diuretic, useful when needed to increase the flow of urine. The fresh leaves have been applied to external wounds to reduce pain and inflammation.

NORTHERN MINER'S CANDLE
Cryptantha celosioides (Eastw.) Payson
Borage Family (Boraginaceae)

Description: This showy wildflower is often called "white forget-me-not" for its resemblance to the closely related blue forget-me-nots (*Myosotis* or *Eritrichium* species). The flowers are tubular at the base, with a flaring throat and 5 limbs (the terminal segments of the petals). The petals are white with a yellow throat. The flower buds are formed in tight, spiraled clusters, like a snail shell. The clusters unwind into a looser arrangement as the flowers bloom. Bristly stiff hair covers the foliage and sepals. The basal leaves are spatula-shaped, with a broad tip, and larger than the leaves higher on the stem. The main central stem is 4–20" tall and is often surrounded by shorter lateral stems.

May–July.

Habitat/Range: Plains, valleys, foothills, and montane forests.

Comments: *Cryptantha* is named from the Greek word *kryptos,* meaning "hidden," and

Northern Miner's Candle

anthos, meaning "flower"; the genus was named from a South American species in which fertilization occurred within the unopened ("hidden") flower.

WHITE MULE'S-EARS
Wyethia helianthoides Nutt.
Aster Family (Asteraceae)

Description: Mule's-ears has both basal leaves (about 9" long and 3" wide) and well-developed stem leaves (about 4" long and 1" wide) arranged alternately on the stems. The leaves of white mule's-ears are covered with thin, long, silky hair. The leafy bracts around the base of the flower head have a fringe of hair on the margin. The large flower heads, 4" in diameter, consist of white to cream-colored ray flowers around the center of yellow disk flowers.

May–June.

Habitat/Range: Meadows in the montane and lower subalpine forests; central and eastern OR, southwestern MT, western WY.

Comments: Yellow and white mule's-ears often hybridize, producing an intermediate offspring with pale yellowish flowers and sparse hair.

White Mule's-Ears

BLACK ELDERBERRY
Sambucus racemosa L.
Honeysuckle Family (Caprifoliaceae)

Description: Black elderberry is a sprawling shrub 3–6' tall with opposite branching. The pinnately compound leaves have 5 (or 7) large leaflets 2–7" long. The stout stems have spongy, reddish brown pith that looks like Styrofoam. The flowers are white to cream colored and are arranged in pyramid-shaped clusters. The fruit is a small, black to dark purple berry, which is borne in dense clusters.

May–July.

Habitat/Range: Streams and open forests of the montane and subalpine zones, especially after a disturbance such as fire.

Comments: Elderberry syrup and wine are well known. However, black elderberry often has a disagreeable taste to many palates, and it is not recommended for eating, whether fresh or made into syrup. The powder-blue berries of blue elderberry (*S. cerulea*) are much more palatable. In any case, the berries of elderberry should not be eaten until fully ripe. The unripe berries, leaves, and stems contain cyanogenic glycosides capable of releasing hydrocyanic acid and causing cyanide poisoning. Children have been poisoned by placing whistles or peashooters made from the green stems into their mouths.

Black Elderberry

Fern-Leaved Candytuft

FERN-LEAVED CANDYTUFT
Smelowskia calycina (Steph.) C. A. Mey.
Mustard Family (Brassicaceae)

Description: This perennial alpine plant is covered with feltlike, soft, dense, light gray hair. Some of the hairs are long and straight while others are shorter and branched. The plants grow in leafy mats on the ground, with flowering stems that reach up to 8" tall. It has compound leaves with 5–9 narrow, pinnately arranged leaf segments. The flowers have 4 white petals, often with a purplish tinge. The fruit is a narrow pod (silique), more than 4 times as long as wide.

May–August.

Habitat/Range: Alpine fellfield.

Comments: *Smelowskia* was named for the Russian botanist Timotheus Smelowsky (1770–1815). The feltlike leaf surface and low growing habit help it to endure the harsh alpine wind.

WHITE CAMPION
Silene latifolia Poiret
(Also *Lycnis alba* Mill.)
Pink Family (Caryophyllaceae)

Description: Although white campion all look very similar, the flowers are actually unisexual, with male flowers appearing on some plants and female flowers on others. Telling them apart requires splitting the sepals in order to see what is hidden inside. The female flower has an ovary with 5 distinct styles (no stamens). The male flower has 10 stamens (no ovary). With a closer look, you will notice the bladdery sepal tube is more inflated in the female flower, and it has more nerves (20) than the male flower (10). Common to both male and female flowers are the white, straplike petals with 2 expanded lobes. The plants are 20-40" tall and are covered with short hairs, and also with sticky glands on at least the upper half. The leaves are opposite, entire, and lance-shaped.

June–August.

Habitat/Range: Introduced; disturbed places, spreading into natural plant communities.

Comments: White campion, like other species

White Campion

of *Silene,* is often called "catchfly." Flies and other insects often get stuck in the glandular hairs on the foliage and are unable to free themselves.

FIELD CHICKWEED
Cerastium arvense L.
Pink Family (Caryophyllaceae)

Description: Field chickweed has stems 2–20"
tall. The stems often trail on the ground, forming mats. The leaves are arranged opposite each
other on the stem. Clusters of secondary leaves,
or leafy shoots, are often crowded in the axils of
the larger, primary leaves. The flowers have 5
styles, 10 stamens, and 5 white, 2-lobed petals
that are about twice as long as the 5 sepals. The
lance-shaped bracts below the flowers, have a
thin, membrane-like margin.

April–August.

Habitat/Range: Valleys to the alpine.

Comments: Field chickweed is most often confused with sandwort (*Arenaria*) and chickweed
(*Stellaria*). However, the flowers of these genera usually have only 3 styles. Also, the petals of
Arenaria species are entire (unlobed), and those

Field Chickweed

of *Stellaria* species are more deeply lobed,
appearing to be 10 separate petals.

PARRY'S CAMPION
Silene parryi (Wats.) Hitch. & Mag.
Pink Family (Caryophyllaceae)

Parry's Campion

Description: Parry's campion has bisexual flowers (both pistil and stamens are present). There
are usually 3 styles on the ovary, but sometimes
there are 4 or even 5. The flower has 10 stamens and 5 white petals that are often greenish
or purple tinged. The blade of each petal has 4
lobes. The tubular, fused portion of the sepals
has 10 prominent purple nerves and 5 teeth.
Glandular hairs cover the surface of the sepals
and the upper part of the foliage. The leaves are
mostly basal, with only 2 (sometimes 3) pairs of
leaves on the flowering stem.

July–August.

Habitat/Range: Rocky slopes in the montane
to the upper subalpine zones; WA, central ID,
WY, MT.

Comments: Parry's campion was named in
honor of Charles Christopher Parry (1823–
1890), a British American botanist and explorer.
Parry worked on the Mexican Boundary Survey from 1849 to 1852 as a geologist and botanist. Later he collected plants in Colorado, Utah,
California, and Mexico. Many plants are named
for him, including Parry's primrose (*Primula
parryi*), Parry's oatgrass (*Danthonia parryi*), and
Parry's townsendia (*Townsendia parryi*).

FIELD BINDWEED
Convolvulus arvensis L.
Morning-Glory Family (Convolvulaceae)

Field Bindweed

Description: The lovely white to pinkish trumpet-shaped flowers of field bindweed disguise the grisly nature of this noxious weed. It is a leafy vine that uses other plants for a trellis, climbing up and often smothering them by excluding the sunlight from their leaves. It has slender underground stems that descend deeply into the soil. The leaves are smooth (hairless) and shaped like an arrowhead. There are 1 or 2 flowers on the end of each primary flower stalk (peduncle), with 2 small, narrow bracts well below the sepals.

April–September.

Habitat/Range: Introduced; disturbed places such as gardens, cropland, and roadsides.

Comments: This plant is very difficult to eliminate or even control once it is established. Cultivation simply breaks up the deep-set underground stems, each segment of which produces a new plant. In many areas of North America it has the reputation of being the worst noxious weed.

BUNCHBERRY
Cornus canadensis L.
Dogwood Family (Cornaceae)

Description: This lovely, low-growing plant of the deep woods has 4 large, white bracts that are often mistaken for the petals. Upon a closer look (with a 10x hand lens) it is apparent that the bracts surround a cluster of tiny flowers, each with 4 petals and 4 stamens. The plants spread on underground stems. There are 4–7 leaves arranged in a whorl (originating from a common point on the stem). The lateral leaf veins are conspicuous, pinnately arranged, and bend to run parallel with the leaf margin.

June–August.

Habitat/Range: Moist, shady forests of the montane and subalpine zones.

Comments: *Cornus* is from a Latin word meaning "horn" or "antler." This may refer to the hard wood of some species. However, ornamental knobs on the ends of ancient manuscript cylinders were also called *Cornus,* suggesting the resemblance with the berry clusters of this plant.

Bunchberry

The berries of bunchberry are edible, being mild and delicate in taste. The plant has been used medicinally as a poultice to treat burns, insect bites, and other skin afflictions.

MERTEN'S MOSS-HEATHER
Cassiope mertensiana (Bong.) G. Don
Heath Family (Ericaceae)

Description: The foliage of Merten's moss-heather has small, scalelike leaves. They are arranged in an opposite pattern, are distinctly 4-ranked, and overlap to completely conceal the stems. The leaves are smooth (hairless) or sometimes have a fringe of short hair on the margin only. The foliage forms low mats on the ground surface. A cluster of white flowers is arranged near the tips of the branches, which are up to 12" tall. The bell-shaped white flowers, with reddish sepals, hang downward.

July–August.

Habitat/Range: Alpine and subalpine forests, WA, northeastern OR, ID, western and south-central MT.

Comments: *Cassiope* is named for a character in Greek mythology. Cassiopeia was the queen of Ethiopia, the wife of King Cepheus. She was vain and boastful, claiming to be more beautiful than the sea nymphs. This angered the sea nymphs, who had Neptune, king of the sea, send the whale Cetus to punish Cassiopeia. Only the

Merten's Moss-Heather

sacrifice of Cassiopeia's daughter, Princess Andromeda, would save the kingdom. In the night sky, the constellation Cassiopeia looks like a *W* in the Milky Way and is often called the "the lady in the chair."

TRAPPER'S TEA
Ledum glandulosum Nutt.
Heath Family (Ericaceae)

Trapper's Tea

Description: Trapper's tea is an evergreen shrub, usually about 3' tall. The leaves are egg-shaped and shiny, dark green on the upper surface, and light green to white on the lower surface. The foliage of trapper's tea has a fragrant aroma when crushed. The twigs are covered with glandular dots and minute hair. The flowers are arranged in open clusters on the ends of the stems. The 5 petals are distinct to the base, not joined together like many other flowers in the heath family.

June–August.

Habitat/Range: Forest wetlands, stream sides.

Comments: The plant is called trapper's tea because of the reported use of the leaves as a beverage by early trappers and settlers. However, this practice could be dangerous. *Ledum,* and several other genera in the heath family, contain adromedotoxin which causes slow pulse, low blood pressure, loss of coordination, convulsions, paralysis, and death. The Delaware Indians used the related eastern mountain laurel in a potion for committing suicide.

DRUMMOND'S MILKVETCH
Astragalus drummondii Doug.
Bean Family (Fabaceae)

Drummond's Milkvetch

Description: Drummond's milkvetch has large white flowers and long, silky hair covering the foliage. The plants are rather stout and about 1–2' tall. The main flower stalk (peduncle) is erect and supports 15–30 flowers. The petals are white or pale yellowish white. The tip of the keel petal is dull lilac. The fruit is a smooth pod that hangs downward even more than the flowers did. In cross section the pod is 3-angled, with 2 lobes.

May–July.

Habitat/Range: Plains, valleys, and foothills; southeastern ID, MT, WY.

Comments: Drummond's milkvetch was named in honor of Thomas Drummond (1780–1835), a Scotch nurseryman and botanist. Drummond was the curator of the Belfast Botanic Garden. Many species of milkvetch are poisonous to livestock, often because of accumulated toxic concentrations of selenium or because they can induce loco disease (see comments for silky crazyweed, *Oxytropis sericea*). Drummond's milkvetch has not been implicated in either of these toxic conditions, but studies are far from complete.

ARCTIC GENTIAN
Gentiana algida Pall.
Gentian Family (Gentianaceae)

Description: The petals of the large arctic gentian flowers are fused together into a funnel-shaped tube, nearly 2" long, with 5 pointed lobes. The flower color is white to pale creamy yellow, streaked and blotched with purple or sometimes green. A rosette of narrow leaves, up to 5" long, forms the plant base. Leafy stems, bearing flowers, rise up to 8" above the basal rosette.

July–September.

Habitat/Range: Alpine bogs, wet meadows, and stream banks; MT, WY.

Comments: The name *algida* comes from the Latin word *algidus* (cold). It is well named, for this gentian only grows in the arctic tundra and on alpine mountaintops with an equivalent cold climate. The blooming of arctic gentian announces that the short summer growing season is winding down.

Arctic Gentian

WHITE FRASERA
Frasera montana Mulford
Gentian Family (Gentianaceae)

Description: White frasera is distinctive with its white-margined opposite leaves and white flowers. It has well-developed basal leaves, while the leaves become progressively smaller up the stem. The flowers are in short, congested clusters on the ends of the 10–20" tall stems. There are 4 sepals, 4 petals, and 4 stamens per flower. Each petal has a broadly oval, depressed gland lined with coarse hair. The petals are uniformly white or cream colored.

Late May–July.

Habitat/Range: Montane forests; central and west-central ID. It is endemic to this area and is found nowhere else in the world.

Comments: *Frasera* was named for the English nurseryman John Fraser (1750–1811). In addition to white frasera, central Idaho is home to a number of other regional endemic plants, including Rocky Mountain paintbrush.

White Frasera

CUSHION MILKVETCH
Astragalus gilviflorus Sheld.
Bean Family (Fabaceae)

Cushion Milkvetch

Description: Cushion milkvetch forms dense, low cushions of silvery gray leaves, each with 3 leaflets. The plants are stemless. The long, white flowers are erect, facing upward from thin, translucent stipules at the base of the leaves. The white banner petal is ⅝–1" long or longer and tapers from near the tip to the base. The short keel petal is normally white with a lilac tip, but it may be purple or blue. The pods are small and inconspicuous.

April–May.

Habitat/Range: Plains, foothills.

Comments: *Gilviflorus* means "dull yellowish-colored flowers." The white flowers of cushion milkvetch turn a dull yellow or yellowish tan color upon drying. The species was first described and named from a dried specimen collected by the Scottish naturalist John Bradbury (1768–1823). Bradbury collected the plant during a botanical expedition to the Mandan villages of North Dakota in 1810–11.

WHITE GERANIUM
Geranium richardsonii Fisch. & Trautv.
Geranium Family (Geraniaceae)

White Geranium

Description: The 5 white petals of the white geranium have pink to purple veins and soft hair about half the length from the petal base. The flower stalks are covered with dense glandular hair, often with reddish tips. The leaves are deeply parted into 5–7 divisions that are coarsely toothed, with a distinctive geranium aroma.

June–August.

Habitat/Range: Montane, subalpine.

Comments: *Geranium* is derived from the Greek word *geranos* (crane). The style of geranium flowers expands into a long beak, like a crane's bill. *Richardsonii* is named in honor of Sir John Richardson (1787–1842), an English surgeon and naturalist. Richardson was the physician on three expeditions to the Arctic and wrote the book *Fauna Boreali-Americana*. Geraniums are medicinal herbs used to treat diarrhea, dysentery, ulcers, and hemorrhoids. It is also used to stop bleeding and reduce the inflammation of minor wounds.

SILVERLEAF PHACELIA
Phacelia hastata Doug. ex Lehm.
Waterleaf Family (Hydrophyllaceae)

Description: This plant has fine, silvery hairs that loosely cover the leaves, giving them a sheen. The leaves are usually entire, but sometimes they have a pair of narrow lobes near the base. The plants have several stems that rise up to 20" from the branched, woody rootstock. The flowers are arranged in compact, spiraled clusters, like a snail shell. The petals are dull white to lavender. The stamens are hairy near the middle and protrude well beyond the flower petals.

May–August.

Habitat/Range: Foothills to alpine.

Comments: *Phacelia* comes from the Greek word *phakelos* (fascicle), which refers to the compact flower arrangement. This species was first described to botanical science from a specimen collected by David Douglas (1799–1834) "on the barren plains of the Columbia." Douglas was a British botanist and early explorer.

Silverleaf Phacelia

STICKY CURRANT
Ribes viscossimum Pursh
Currant Family (Grossulariaceae)

Description: This medium-sized shrub (to 6' tall) is unarmed, without the thorns or prickles of some gooseberries and currants. However, it is covered with glandular hairs that are sticky to the touch and give the plant its characteristic aroma. The flowers are greenish white to yellowish white and often tinged with pink. The flower tube is bell-shaped and attached to the top of the ovary. The lobes of the sepals and petals (5 each) flare from the end of the "bell." The leaves are maplelike, with palmate veins (that radiate from the leaf base) and rounded lobes.

May–August.

Habitat/Range: Montane and subalpine forest.

Comments: *Viscosissimum* comes from the Latin word *viscidus,* meaning "sticky."

Sticky Currant

MOCKORANGE
Philadelphus lewisii Pursh
Hydrangea Family (Hydrangeaceae)

Description: This is an erect shrub, up to 9' tall and densely branched. On older stems the reddish brown bark cracks open at a right angle to the stem and eventually falls away in small pieces, revealing the gray bark underneath. The leaves are in pairs, opposite each other on the stems. Each flower has 4 petals, many stamens, 4 styles, and a sweet orange-blossom aroma. The fruit is a hard capsule that remains on the shrub through the winter.

May–July.

Habitat/Range: Rocky hillsides, rock crevices, and stream banks; WA, OR, ID, MT.

Comments: Mockorange is the state flower of Idaho, where it is often called syringa. The name *philadelphus* was derived from the Greek *philos* (love) and *adelphos* (brother). In 1814, Frederick Pursh named the plant *Philadelphus lewisii* in honor of Meriwether Lewis, from specimens that Lewis collected in 1806: one on May 6, along the Clearwater River in Idaho, and another along the Blackfoot River of Montana on July 4.

Mockorange

Nodding Onion

NODDING ONION
Allium cernuum Roth
Lily Family (Liliaceae)

Description: The flower heads of this small herb bend downward. The flowers are arranged in a simple umbel, with the individual flower stalks coming together at a common point on the end of a leafless stem 4–20" tall. The 6 tepals (petals and petal-like sepals) are white to pink and are separate all the way to the base. The 6 stamens and the style extend well beyond the tepals. The leaves are flat to concave in cross section, and solid (not hollow). The entire plant has a distinctly oniony aroma.

June–July.

Habitat/Range: Grasslands, sagebrush steppes, and dry, open forests from the valleys to the montane forests.

Comments: *Allium* is the classical name for garlic. All true onion and garlic species fall in this genus. *Cernuum* means "drooping" or "nodding." Twenty-seven species of native onions occur in the Pacific Northwest; some are rare endemics. All onion species are both edible and valuable medicinal herbs. However, digging their bulbs for food kills them. If tempted to sample onions when out in the backcountry, try using the leaves, much as you would chives. Gather carefully so as not to remove all the leaves of any one plant.

Geyer's Onion

GEYER'S ONION
Allium geyeri Wats.
Lily Family (Liliaceae)

Description: The flower cluster (umbel) of Geyer's onion is erect. The flowers are pink to white. The 6 stamens are hidden by the longer tepals (petals and petal-like sepals). The tips of the tepals are sharply pointed and erect. In the Central Rocky Mountains, many of the flowers in the floral cluster are replaced by small, stalkless bulbs clustered at the base. These bulbs are a means of asexual reproduction; they fall to the ground and sprout, clones of the parent plant. Plants with bulbs in the flower cluster are in the variety *tenerum,* while those without are in the variety *geyeri.* The main stalk supporting the flower cluster is leafless and 4–20" tall. The 3 (or more) leaves rise from the base of the stalk.

These leaves are concave to convex in cross section and solid.

May–June.

Habitat/Range: Wet meadows and along stream sides in the montane and subalpine forests. The variety *tenerum* is common in the region; the variety *geyeri* is found in northern ID and eastern WA.

Comments: Geyer's onion was named in honor of Carl Andreas Geyer (1809–1853), a German botanist who collected plants in the Missouri River region and Oregon Territory. The flowers of Geyer's onion (and most others) begin blooming from the perimeter of the floral umbel, and progress toward the center. Siberian chives (which often co-occurs) first blooms in the center, and progresses outward to the perimeter.

BIG-POD MARIPOSA LILY
Calochortus eurycarpus Wats.
Lily Family (Liliaceae)

Big-Pod Mariposa Lily

Description: Mariposa lilies have 3 narrow, green sepals and 3 broad, bright petals. The petals are primarily creamy white to lavender and have fringed glands on the inner surface. The fringed gland of big-pod mariposa lily is shaped like a crescent or half-moon. Well above the gland, in the center of the petal, is a large, roundish, purple spot. The ovary is 3-winged, expanding in fruit to a large, dry capsule with 3 broad wings. The basal leaf is long and narrow, like a grass leaf, but much shorter than the flower stalk. A few shorter leafy bracts are on the stem.

June–August.

Habitat/Range: Open forests and grasslands; southwestern MT, western WY, central ID, and the Blue Mountains of WA and OR.

Comments: The name was derived from the Greek words *kalo* (beautiful) and *chortos* (grass). *Eurycarpus* comes from the Greek prefix *eu-* (good; well-developed) and *carpos* (fruit). So, *Calochortus eurycarpus* is "the beautiful grass with well-developed fruit." *Mariposa* is Spanish for "butterfly."

GUNNISON'S MARIPOSA LILY
Calochortus gunnisonii S. Wats.
Lily Family (Liliaceae)

Description: Gunnison's mariposa lily has branched and gland-tipped hairs on the surface of the petals. The fringed gland on the petal is oblong. There is a narrow purple band immediately above the gland and a purple spot below it. The purple band and spot are repeated on the 3 sepals. The 3 petals vary from white to purple or occasionally yellow. There are several linear, grasslike leaves on the stem. The largest leaf is at the base. The others get progressively smaller upward on the stem. The capsule is a narrow pod, triangular in cross section, but not at all winged.

June–August.

Habitat/Range: Grasslands and open woods from valleys to the montane forests; MT, WY.

Comments: This plant was named Gunnison's mariposa lily for John Howard Gunnison, commander of the 1853 expedition to survey a road from Colorado to Salt Lake City. Gunnison was killed by Indians in Utah while leading the expedition. This species, collected by an expedi-

Gunnison's Mariposa Lily

tion botanist, was named in Gunnison's honor. Mariposa lily is sometimes called star lily or sego lily. (Remember the flower on the label of Sego brand canned milk?) In the spring of 1848, Native Americans showed the starving Mormons how to dig them for food. The Mormons consider the sego lily to be a symbol of life and hope; it is the Utah state flower.

FALSE SOLOMON'S SEAL

Smilacina racemosa (L.) Desf.
Lily Family (Liliaceae)

Description: False solomon's seal has erect, unbranched stems about 2' tall with numerous leaves. The leaves are egg-shaped or even more oblong, with an abruptly pointed tip. The numerous tiny flowers are arranged in a branching panicle, upright on the end of the branches. The flowers have 6 creamy white floral tepals (petals and petal-like sepals), and 6 stamens. The fruit is a red berry flecked with purple, becoming more uniformly red when fully ripe.

April–July.

Habitat/Range: Under the canopy of trees or tall shrubs in the montane and lower subalpine forests.

Comments: *Smilacina* means "a small *Smilax*," named for its resemblance to plants in the catbrier family. *Racemosa* implies that the plant has a simple branched raceme flower arrangement, but actually the flowers are arranged in a many-branched panicle. True "solomon's seal" are plants in the genus *Polygonatum* (also in the lily

False Solomon's Seal

family) and grow east of the Rocky Mountains. Because of their resemblance and confusion with *Polygonatum* species, the name "false solomon's seal" was coined and applied to *Smilacina* species.

FAIRY-BELLS

Disporum trachycarpum (Wats.) Benth.
   & Hook.
Lily Family (Liliaceae)

Fairy-Bells

Description: Fairy-bells flowers hang down from the ends of the branches, often concealed under the broad leaves. There are usually 2 creamy white, bell-shaped flowers per branch, but sometimes 1 or 3. Each flower has 6 separate and similar tepals (petals and petal-like sepals) and 6 stamens. The leaves are egg-shaped, abruptly pointed on the end, with a fringe of hair on the margin. The parallel leaf veins are conspicuous. The branched stems are brown and woody in appearance. The fruit is a round, bright red berry with numerous (6–12) seeds.

May–July.

Habitat/Range: Montane forests.

Comments: *Disporum* is derived from the Greek *dis* (double) and *spora* (seed), perhaps because of the two berries typical of the genus. *Trachycarpum* is also from Greek roots, meaning "rough fruit." The surface of the berry is warty and covered with minute nipplelike projections. These berries are edible, mild, and taste faintly like cantaloupe.

WILD LILY-OF-THE-VALLEY
Smilacina stellata (L.) Desf.
Lily Family (Liliaceae)

Wild Lily-of-the-Valley

Description: Wild lily-of-the-valley has its flowers arranged in a few-flowered (5–10 flowers), simple raceme. The stem is distinctly "zigzag" in design. The flowers have 3 sepals, 3 petals, and 6 stamens. The berries are greenish yellow, with 3 red stripes, aging to red or black. *May–June.*

Habitat/Range: Valleys to the subalpine.

Comments: This common native wildflower was named for its resemblance to the introduced garden flower, lily-of-the-valley (*Convallaria majalis*), which has bell-shaped and nodding flowers. These garden plants have dangerously poisonous compounds that are purgative and have a digitalis-like effect on the heart, disturbing the heartbeat and pulse. Our native wild lily-of-the-valley has edible berries, although they are not very tasty, and eating too many will unleash their laxative properties. It is sometimes called starry solomon's seal.

TWISTED STALK
Streptopus amplexifolius (L.) DC.
Lily Family (Liliaceae)

Description: The flowers of twisted stalk hide under the leaves, 1 flower per leaf. An unusual kink or twist in the flower stalk is the key distinguishing feature. The flowers have 6 white to greenish yellow floral tepals (petals and petal-like sepals) and 6 stamens. The fruit is a red (or yellow) berry with a smooth, tender skin. The stems are stout, erect, and branched and stand 1–3' tall. The leaves are broad and are heart-shaped at the base where they clasp the stem. *May–July.*

Habitat/Range: Montane and subalpine streams.

Comments: *Streptopus* is from the Greek roots *streptos* (twisted) and *pous* (foot). *Amplexifolius* refers to the clasping leaves. The berries are edible and very mild in flavor. The green shoots may be eaten raw and are said to taste like cucumber. However, the young leaves could lead one to confuse this plant with false hellebore, a dangerous poisonous plant.

Twisted Stalk

STICKY TOFIELDIA
Tofieldia glutinosa (Michx.) Pers.
Lily Family (Liliaceae)

Description: Except for the flower head, this plant looks much like a grass. The leaves are long, narrow, 2-ranked, and folded to sheath the stem, like grasses. Above the leaves the stem is densely covered with short glandular hair. The plants are slender and 4–20" tall. At the top of the stem is a dense cluster of white to greenish flowers. If you look carefully you will see that the flowers are arranged in groups of 3 within the cluster. Each flower has 6 floral tepals (petals and petal-like sepals) and 6 stamens. The fruit is a 3-lobed capsule.

June–August.

Habitat/Range: Wet meadows, streams, and ponds of subalpine forests.

Sticky Tofieldia

Comments: *Tofieldia* was named in honor of the English botanist Thomas Tofield (1730–1779). *Glutinosa* means "sticky," referring to the glandular hairs on the stem that are sticky to the touch. Mosquitoes, common in the habitat of *Tofieldia*, are often trapped on the sticky stems, which are like flypaper.

BEARGRASS
Xerophyllum tenax (Pursh) Nutt.
Lily Family (Liliaceae)

Description: Beargrass consists of a dense clump of long, wiry, grasslike leaves and the dense cluster of small white flowers on a tall stalk. The leaves are evergreen and long-lived, remaining on the plant for several years. The margin of the leaf has short bristly hairs that are rough to the touch. Basal leaves are 1–2' or more in length. The leaves on the stem get progressively shorter upward. Each flower has 6 narrow floral tepals (petals and petal-like sepals) and 6 stamens. The plants do not bloom every year, and the dead stalks often remain on them as a testament to the last flowering.

May–August.

Habitat/Range: Well-drained areas of the montane and subalpine forests zones.

Comments: *Xerophyllum* is derived from Greek words meaning "dry leaf." A specimen was collected by Meriwether Lewis on June 15, 1806, east of Weippe Prairie, Idaho. Lewis mentioned the plant many times in his journals. He was especially impressed with the ability of the Native Americans to weave watertight baskets and conical hats from the leaves of beargrass and cedar bark.

Beargrass

TRILLIUM
Trillium ovatum Pursh
Lily Family (Liliaceae)

Description: The 3 large, broadly egg-shaped leaves of trillium are very distinctive. They are arranged in a whorl, that is, attached to the stem at a common point. A single flower normally blooms a few inches above the whorl of leaves. The flower has 3 green sepals, 3 white petals, 6 stamens, and 3 long stigma lobes. As the flower ages the petals turn from white to pink and finally purple.

March–June.

Habitat/Range: Boggy areas in montane and subalpine forests; more common in the Northern Rockies than the Central Rockies.

Comments: This species was named *Trillium* for the 3 leaves (and sepals, petals, stigmas) and *ovatum* for the ovate (egg-shaped) leaf shape. Trillium is also called wake-robin, because trilliums and robins appear at about the same time in early spring. It is also called birth-root because it was used by Native American women to reduce uterine bleeding during childbirth. The Chippewa Indians used trillium for rheumatism and cramps. Herbalists claim that species of *Trillium* are a tonic for the uterus and useful in reducing excessive blood flow during menses.

Trillium

YUCCA
Yucca glauca Nutt.
Lily Family (Liliaceae)
(Also Agave Family [Agavaceae])

Description: With its dense clump of sharply pointed basal leaves and persistent, large, woody pods, yucca is unmistakable. The stiff, narrow leaves are blue-green and glaucous (covered with a fine powdery substance that rubs off). The flowers are large (2" long), with 6 broad floral tepals (petals and petal-like sepals) and 6 stamens.

May–July.

Habitat/Range: Plains, mountain valleys, and foothills, often on sandy, well-drained sites; MT, WY.

Comments: Pollination of yucca flowers is an incredible example of symbiosis involving a plant and an insect. A night-flying moth (*Tegeticula* or *Pronuba* species) enters the flower, pierces the ovary, and lays its eggs deep inside, among the ovules. Then it crawls up to the anther and collects a mass of pollen. The next stop is the stigma, where the moth pushes the pollen deep into the stigmatic funnel, ensuring successful pollination. The fertilized ovules then develop

Yucca

into many seeds; although these are food for the developing insects, there are more seeds than they can eat. Look at the yucca capsules to find the hole where the larvae chewed their way to freedom.

SHOWY DEATH-CAMAS
Zigadenus elegans Pursh
Lily Family (Liliaceae)

Description: Death-camas species have a distinctive gland near the base of the 6 floral tepals (petals and petal-like sepals). The glands of showy death-camas are deeply lobed and heart-shaped. The petals are egg-shaped, ¼" long or longer, and rather large. There are 3 distinct styles that persist as beaks on the dry capsule. The greenish white flowers are arranged in a raceme. The leaves are long and narrow, mostly basal.

June–August.

Habitat/Range: Montane to alpine.

Comments: Showy death-camas is a poisonous plant, responsible for the deaths of both livestock and humans. Human poisoning has most often occurred when the bulbs were mistaken for the edible meadow camas.

Showy Death-Camas

SPOTTED CORALROOT
Corallorhiza maculata Raf.
Orchid Family (Orchidaceae)

Spotted Coralroot

Description: Spotted coralroot lacks green leaves. Clothed with membranous bracts that sheath the stems, the plants are reddish purple to brownish purple. A raceme of 10–30 dainty flowers adorns the top of the stem. The 3 sepals and 2 upper petals are reddish purple. The lip petal is white with dark red spots and 2 lateral lobes. Occasionally, one encounters an albino plant, which is pale yellow with white flowers that lack the purple spots.

June–July.

Habitat/Range: Organic humus layer of shady woods in the montane and lower subalpine forests.

Comments: Spotted coralroot does not produce food by photosynthesis, but rather lives in a complex relationship with soil fungi. The coral-like rhizomes (underground stems) gather nutrients from tree roots and rotting humus by parasitizing fungi that take up residence in the spongy tissue of the rhizomes. The fungus initially invades the orchid seed coat. The orchid embryo neutralizes the attack by the fungus and through a complex chemical exchange establishes a life-long and mutually beneficial relationship with the fungus.

GUMBO EVENING-PRIMROSE
Oenothera caespitosa Nutt.
Evening-Primrose Family (Onagraceae)

Gumbo Evening-Primrose

Description: The flowers of gumbo evening-primrose grow close to the ground from the center of a cluster of radiating basal leaves. The flowers have 4 petals that are white when fresh but turn pink and purple as they age. The 4 sepals turn back toward the stem, away from the petals. There are 8 stamens. The anthers are attached to the filaments in the center, where they turn freely. There are 4 prominent stigma lobes on the end of the style.

May–July.

Habitat/Range: Plains and valleys to the alpine zone.

Comments: A gumbo evening-primrose flower is short-lived. Its flowers open near sunset and wilt the next day. During the night, the white flowers and sweet nectar attract nocturnal hawkmoths for pollination. Meriwether Lewis collected a specimen of this plant "near the falls of the Missouri, 17th July 1806."

MOUNTAIN LADY'S-SLIPPER
Cypripedium montanum Dougl. ex Lindl.
Orchid Family (Orchidaceae)

Description: The flowers of mountain lady's-slipper are almost identical to yellow lady's-slipper, except for the color. The white lip petal is inflated and pouchlike, but without the flat platform in front of the pouch found on fairy slipper (*Calypso bulbosa*). A few purple stripes or spots often decorate the white lip, especially within the pouch. The sepals and lateral petals are brownish purple, twisted, and wavy. There is a large green leafy bract attached to the stem just below the flower. The leaves are about 2–6" long, about half as wide, and strongly parallel veined. The plants are up to 2' tall.

May–early July.

Habitat/Range: Under the open canopy of trees or tall shrubs in montane forests.

Comments: Meriwether Lewis mentioned this plant in his journal on June 30, 1806, as the expedition was descending Lolo Creek in present-day Montana. He wrote: "I also met with the plant in blume which is sometimes called the lady's slipper or mockerson flower. it is in shape and appearance like ours only that the corolla is

Mountain Lady's Slipper

white, marked with small veigns of pale red longitudinally on the inner side. after dinner we resumed our march."

WHITE BOG ORCHID
Habenaria dilatata (Pursh) Hook.
(Also *Platanthera dilatata* (Pursh) Lind.)
Orchid Family (Orchidaceae)

Description: White flowers, and the abruptly expanded base of the lip petal, help to distinguish this species from the similar northern green bog orchid and related species. There are several (more than 4) leaves on the stem, which get progressively smaller up the stem. The plants are slender and sometimes 3' tall or more. The lip petal has a spur that is about the same length as the lip, but it can vary from twice to half as long. The flowers have a pleasant and distinctive fragrance.

June–August.

Habitat/Range: Bogs, wet meadows, and along the shores of streams and ponds from the valleys to subalpine forests.

Comments: Bog orchids are included in the genus *Habenaria* or *Platanthera,* depending on the floral manual consulted. *Habenaria* is derived from the Latin *habena* or "reins," referring to the reinlike appendages of the lip of some

White Bog Orchid

species. *Dilatata* means "dilated," which refers to the expanded base of the lip of white bog orchid.

Small Round-Leaved Orchis

SMALL ROUND-LEAVED ORCHIS
Orchis rotundifolia Banks ex Pursh
(Also *Amerorchis rotundifolia* (Banks) Hul.)
Orchid Family (Orchidaceae)

Description: Small round-leaved orchis has a single basal leaf that is oval or almost round. The leafless stem is usually about 6" tall. About 2–8 flowers are arranged in a loose raceme on the end of the stem. The petals and sepals range from white to pink. The lip has 3 prominent lobes and a slender spur. The blade of the lip is dotted or streaked with purple.

June–July.

Habitat/Range: Limestone springs in coniferous wetlands; northern Continental Divide in MT, northwestern WY.

Comments: *Amerorchis* means "the orchis from America," and *rotundifolia* means "round-leaved." Small round-leaved orchis is rare in the Central Rocky Mountains, since it is peripheral to the main body of the population and at times totally isolated (disjunct) from it.

Hooded ladies'-Tresses

HOODED LADIES'-TRESSES
Spiranthes romanzoffiana Cham.
Orchid Family (Orchidaceae)

Description: As many as 60 densely spaced, white flowers coil around the end of the stem in 3 spiraling ranks. The stems are 4–24" tall. They have numerous narrow leaves on the lower half, which give way to small bracts above. The sepals and upper petals jut forward, while the lip petal turns sharply downward. The base of the lip petal is narrow, and the apex is wider, with fine teeth or tears on the margin.

July–August.

Habitat/Range: Wetlands; plains to subalpine.

Comments: *Spiranthes* comes from the Greek *speira* (coil) and *anthos* (flower), which describes the coiled flower arrangement. Named *romozoffiana* in honor of Nicholas Romanzoff (1754–1826), a Russian minister of state. The species was discovered on the Aleutian island of Unalaska, while Alaska was Russian territory.

COMMON PLANTAIN
Plantago major L.
Plantain Family (Plantaginaceae)

Description: This is a perennial plant with large basal leaves (about 5" long and 3" wide). The plants are sometimes called "ribgrass" because of the prominent, parallel veins of the leaf. The leafless stem is about 6" tall, with a dense, narrow, cylindrical flower arrangement on the end. The numerous flowers are tiny and unnoticeable without a hand lens. The petals are thin, dry, and turn downward on the end. The 4 stamens extend well beyond the petals.

May–August.

Habitat/Range: Introduced; disturbed places from the valleys to the montane forests.

Comments: Native Americans used plantain externally to treat wounds and infections and to draw out thorns or splinters. It was also taken internally for colds and various stomach complaints. A commonly used bulk laxative is made from the seed of *Plantago psyllium.* Herbalists

Common Plantain

have long relied on common plantain leaves for soothing inflamed mucous membranes, such as sore throats and hemorrhoids.

FRINGED GRASS-OF-PARNASSUS

Parnassia fimbriata Koenig
Grass-of-Parnassus Family (Parnassiaceae)
(Also Saxifrage Family [Saxifragaceae])

Description: The flowers of fringed grass-of-parnassus are garnished with a conspicuous tasseled border on the lower half of the 5 petals. Staminodes (infertile stamens), opposite the petals, look like strange little paws (with a 10x hand lens). The flowers also have 5 fertile, normal-looking stamens alternate with the petals. The 5 sepals (underneath the petals) have fine, irregular teeth toward the tip. The stems are 4–14" long. They have a single small leaf on the upper half and a single flower on the end. The rest of the leaves are all basal and kidney-shaped. *June–October.*

Habitat/Range: Wetlands from montane forests to timberline in the subalpine zone.

Comments: *Parnassia* is named for Mount Parnassus in central Greece. Grass-of-Parnassus was first recorded from there by Dioscorides, a military physician for Nero, the emperor of

Fringed Grass-of-Parnassus

Rome in the first century A.D. Dioscorides wrote *Materia Medica,* which was a description of about 600 species that he used for medicinal purposes—one of the earliest botanical works known.

BALL-HEAD GILIA

Ipomopsis congesta (Hook.) Grant
(Also *Gilia congesta* Hook.)
Phlox Family (Polemoniaceae)

Description: These plants have a dense flower arrangement that is almost round, like a ball. Each flower has a tube that is expanded into 5 lobes. The flowers are white and sometimes flecked with purple. The sepals are also tubular at the base, with 5 sharply pointed lobes. The stamens are visible, just inside the throat of the petals. The filaments are longer than the anthers. The leaves are usually deeply divided, with several to many narrow segments. One variety of the species in the Central Rocky Mountains (var. *crebrifolia*) has entire leaves (not segmented or lobed). The leaves and stems are covered with white, dense, woolly hair. The leaves are usually concentrated at the base of the plant and are more widely spaced on the stem.

June–August.

Habitat/Range: Dry, open places from the prairies and valleys to montane and alpine zones.

Comments: The variety *montana* is a trifoliate (3 leaflets per leaf), mat-forming plant of alpine areas in California and Nevada. In contrast, the variety *congesta* is a more upright plant with pinnately divided leaves, found in the plains, valleys, and lower mountains of the Central Rocky Mountains.

Ball-Head Gilia

LONG-LEAVED PHLOX
Phlox longifolia Nutt.
Phlox Family (Polemoniaceae)

Description: The long leaves and loose, erect stems of long-leaved phlox are distinctive. The

Long-Leaved Phlox

larger leaves are 1–3" long or more. The plants are usually 4" or more tall, unless flattened by the wind. They do not form the compact mats of many other phlox species in the Central Rocky Mountains. The flowers have a well-developed slender pedicel (flower stalk). The petals range from white to pink. The sepals have 5 prominent, slender teeth that lead to ribs on the sepal tube. Toward the base of the sepal tube there is a distinctive bulge between the ribs (visible with a hand lens).

April–July.

Habitat/Range: Dry, open, often rocky places from the plains and valleys to the montane forests.

Comments: Native Americans used long-leaved phlox for building the blood in anemic children and for treating eye problems, stomachache, diarrhea, and venereal disease.

SULPHUR BUCKWHEAT
Eriogonum umbellatum Torr.
Buckwheat Family (Polygonaceae)

Description: The basal leaves of sulphur buckwheat often form large, flat mats up to 2' wide. The leaves are green on the upper surface. Dense woolly hair on the lower surface gives it a grayish white color. The woolly flowering stems are 2–12" tall, with an umbel (umbrellalike) flower arrangement. A whorl of leafy bracts radiates from just below the common junction of the rays (branches) of the umbels. The individual flowers are on a long, slender pedicel (flower stalk) that is attached within a cup-shaped bract with 3–10 downturned lobes. The tepals (petals and petal-like sepals) are smooth (hairless) on the back. They vary from creamy white to yellow and are often tinged with red or purple, especially as they age.

June–August.

Habitat/Range: Plains and mountain valleys to the alpine zone.

Comments: *Eriogonum* comes from the Greek roots *erion* (wool) and *gony* (knee), probably

Sulphur Buckwheat

because of the woolly hair on the stems. Various Native American tribes used buckwheat species for treating colds, tuberculosis, rheumatism, stomach trouble, diarrhea, bleeding, sore eyes, and as a diuretic.

CUSHION PHLOX
Phlox pulvinata (Wherry) Cronq.
Phlox Family (Polemoniaceae)

Cushion Phlox

Description: Cushion phlox is a low, mat-forming plant about 2 ½" tall or less. The leaves are narrow, linear, and sharply pointed. There is a fringe of short hair on the leaf margin, at least toward the base. The surface of the leaves is often hairy, glandular, or both. The flowers have a slender tube and 5 abruptly spreading lobes. The 5 stamens are attached just inside the tube. The style is usually less than ¼" long. The flowers are usually white but are sometimes pale blue.

June–August.

Habitat/Range: Subalpine, alpine.

Comments: *Phlox* is from a Greek root meaning "flame," for the bright colors of some species. *Pulvinata* means "cushionlike." The several low-growing phlox species of the Central Rocky Mountains are difficult to separate.

BANEBERRY
Actaea rubra (Ait.) Willd.
Buttercup Family (Ranunculaceae)

Baneberry

Description: The white berries are said to resemble "doll's eyes," and the plants that bear them are often referred to by that name. The "eye" is the dark, persistent stigma on the berry. Botanists have shown that both white- and red-berried forms are in the same species. When in bloom, 25 or more small white flowers are arranged in a large cluster at the end of the stem. A close look at a flower will show that there is only a single style, numerous stamens with long filaments, 5–10 cream-colored petals, and 3–5 whitish petal-like sepals. The leaves are large and compound, with 9 or more toothed leaflets, often in groups of 3.

May–July.

Habitat/Range: Wet forested areas, under the canopy of trees and shrubs and beside streams.

Comments: *Actaea* is the Greek name for "elderberry," which has some superficial similarities in leaf and fruit to baneberry, but which is not closely related. *Bane* means "poison" or "death"; baneberry has poisonous berries that cause severe intestinal inflammation. There are reports of children who have died after eating the berries.

SPRINGBEAUTY
Claytonia lanceolata Pursh
Purslane Family (Portulacaceae)

Description: The flowers of springbeauty appear pink because of the reddish veins of the petals and pink anthers. The tips of the petals

Springbeauty

COLORADO COLUMBINE
Aquilegia coerulea E. James
Buttercup Family (Ranunculaceae)

Description: The white (or blue) flowers of Colorado columbine have 5 long spurs. The spurs are rather straight and exceptionally long (1–3"). The basal leaves are twice ternately compound (3 x 3), that is, with 9 leaflets per leaf. Leaves on the flowering stem are much smaller than the basal leaves and are often reduced to bracts. The flowering stems are up to 2½' tall, much taller than the basal leaves.

Late June–August.

Habitat/Range: Cool, moist places in the subalpine forests; south-central MT, southeastern ID, western WY.

Comments: Colorado columbine is the official state flower of Colorado and is protected there by law. Hummingbirds and hawkmoths often pollinate the flowers; both are able to reach the nectar deep in the long spurs. There are 4 uncommon species of columbine in the Rocky Mountains that also have white to blue flowers, which could be confused with Colorado columbine. However, these columbines have spurs that

are distinctly notched. There are only 2 green sepals, but there are 5 petals, 5 stamens, and 3 styles. The leaves are lance-shaped and opposite. The plants are usually less than 8" tall. Yellow springbeauty (*Claytonia flava*) was once considered to be a variety of *C. lanceolata*. However, yellow springbeauty differs by having narrower leaves and petals that lack the notch or pink veins. The petals of yellow springbeauty may be yellow, but they are more often white and turn yellow upon drying.

Habitat/Range: Cool, moist soil of recent snow melts from the valleys to the alpine zone.

Comments: Springbeauty is in the same family as the bitterroot (*Lewisia rediviva*), and Native Americans used both for food. All parts of the plant are edible, fresh or cooked. It is also a favorite food of pocket gophers, black bears, and grizzly bears, and it is rightfully left for them.

Colorado Columbine

are much shorter (½" or less) and three of them have spurs that are hook-shaped, not long and straight like those of Colorado columbine.

MARSH-MARIGOLD
Caltha leptosepala DC.
Buttercup Family (Ranunculaceae)

Description: The leaves of marsh-marigold are simple, longer than broad, with a heart-shaped base, that is, shaped like an arrowhead with a rounded point. The margin of the leaf has blunt or rounded teeth, especially on the lower half. Most of the leaves are basal. Sometimes there is a single leaf near the base of the otherwise leafless stem. A single large flower is on the end of the stem. There are 5–12 petal-like sepals, no true petals, and many stamens. The sepals are white or yellowish and are tinged with blue on the back.

Late May–August.

Habitat/Range: Wet places in the subalpine and alpine zones.

Comments: The leaves of some species of *Caltha* have been eaten in Europe and eastern North America, but only after boiling in several changes of water to remove the bitter taste. Like many other plants in the buttercup family,

Marsh-Marigold

marsh-marigold has poisonous, acrid juice capable of blistering the mucous membranes if eaten raw.

Water Buttercup

WATER BUTTERCUP
Ranunculus aquatilis L.
Buttercup Family (Ranunculaceae)

Description: Water buttercup is notable for the dense clumps of threadlike leaves submerged in the water and for the white flowers floating on the surface. Some plants also have broader, 3-parted leaves floating on the surface, in addition to the threadlike submerged leaves. Other plants have only the threadlike leaves, which at times seem so dense as to almost clog the stream. Whether threadlike or not, the leaves have a distinct petiole (leaf stalk) and will collapse when removed from the water. The flowers have 5 sepals, 5–10 white petals, and 10–15 stamens and pistils.

May–August.

Habitat/Range: Sluggish streams, ponds, and lakes.

Comments: Water buttercup is important cover for small fish and is a productive substrate for the invertebrate aquatic life that fish feed on.

BUCKBRUSH CEANOTHUS
Ceanothus velutinus Dougl. ex Hook
Buckthorn Family (Rhamnaceae)

Buckbrush Ceanothus

Description: Buckbrush ceanothus is a medium-sized, evergreen shrub 2–6' tall, with shiny, dark green, aromatic leaves. The leaves have 3 prominent veins that radiate from the leaf base. A varnishlike sticky substance on the upper leaf surface gives it a shiny appearance and its strong, characteristic aroma. The lower leaf surface is dull gray. The leaves are arranged alternately on the rather stiff, woody stems. Flower parts are in groups of 5, except for the single pistil with a 3-lobed stigma. The fruit is a hard capsule that separates into 3 segments upon maturing.

June–August.

Habitat/Range: Well-drained mountain slopes in the montane and subalpine zones. It is especially abundant after a forest fire or other disturbance.

Comments: "Red root" is the name often used for this plant by herbalists, who rely on the herb to improve lymphatic and capillary health and to treat inflammation of the throat, tonsils, and sinuses. Native Americans of the Great Lakes region used New Jersey tea (*Ceanothus americanus*) for stomach problems and snakebite.

MOUNTAIN AVENS
Dryas octopetala L.
Rose Family (Rosaceae)

Description: The evergreen leaves are dark green on the upper surface. Underneath they are covered with white, woolly hair. The margins of the leaves are rolled under toward the lower side, and lined with rounded teeth. The leafless stem bears a single white flower. The 8–10 sepals are covered with soft, woolly hair and purplish black glands. There are also 8–10 petals and numerous stamens and pistils.

Late June–August.

Habitat/Range: Alpine tundra.

Comments: *Dryas* is named for the mythical dryads, or wood nymphs, probably because the leaves resemble tiny oak leaves. Cushion plants like *Dryas* are adapted to life in the high wind and desertlike conditions of the fellfield. The constant wind sweeps the snow from these slopes and rapidly evaporates what moisture is left.

Mountain Avens

Western Serviceberry

WESTERN SERVICEBERRY
Amelanchier alnifolia (Nutt.) Nutt. ex Roem.
Rose Family (Rosaceae)

Description: These are often stately shrubs, up to 30' tall, but are more often less than half that size in the Central Rocky Mountains. On drier sites, and where trimmed by browsing animals, they may remain 3' or less. The stems are alternately branched. The larger stems have smooth gray bark, while the twigs of the current year are reddish brown. The base of the leaf is rounded, with a smooth margin. The upper half of the leaf margin is coarsely toothed. The young leaves have silky hair, at least on the lower surface. The flowers are arranged in 5–15 flower racemes on the ends of the twigs. The 5 white petals are rather long and showy, widest above the middle and tapering to a narrow base. The purple fruit looks like a blueberry, but is technically more like an apple.

May–July.

Habitat/Range: Plains and valleys up to the subalpine forests.

Comments: *Amelanchier* was adapted from the French name for a European species. *Alnifolia* means "leaves like an alder." Serviceberry (or sarvisberry) is also called saskatoon, shadbush, or juneberry. The berries were widely used by Native American people, who pounded them into large cakes, which were dried for storage or mixed with dried meat to make pemmican. Serviceberry is an important browse plant for deer and elk.

AMERICAN PLUM
Prunus americana Marsh.
Rose Family (Rosaceae)

Description: The spine-tipped branches and few (2–5) flowered racemes easily distinguish

American Plum

American plum from chokecherry and other *Prunus* species in the Central Rocky Mountains. The plants form dense thickets 9–24' tall that spread by suckering. The alternately arranged leaves are lance-shaped with sharp, forward-pointing teeth on the margin. The white flowers are formed on the tip of smooth (hairless) spur branches, usually before the leaves appear. The flower has a superior ovary with a single style, 5 sepals, 5 petals, and numerous stamens (20 or more). The fruit is about 1" long, red to yellow, with yellow flesh. It has a single stone that is longer than wide.

April–May.

Habitat/Range: Stream banks and woody draws of plains, foothills, and valleys; MT, WY.

Comments: *Prunus* is the ancient Latin name for the plum. The Native Americans of the Great Plains used wild plum medicinally to treat diarrhea, canker sores, and stomach problems. Young twigs were used to prepare a prayer wand for the sick.

THIMBLEBERRY
Rubus parviflorus Nutt.
Rose Family (Rosaceae)

Description: The large maplelike leaves and red, thumb-sized fruit of this shrub are familiar along forest trails in the Central Rocky Mountains. The shrubs are unarmed, without the thorns and prickles of the closely related red and blackcap raspberries (*Rubus* species). The older stems are 2–6' tall, with loose bark that peels off in long strips. The white flowers are 1–2" in diameter and are arranged in 3–7-flowered racemes. The fruit is an aggregate of fleshy, one-seeded segments that loosen and fall from the receptacle when ripe.

June–August.

Habitat/Range: Streams and shady, moist woods of the montane and subalpine forests.

Comments: *Rubus* is the Latin name for "bramble" and is related to *ruber* (red). The fruits are juicy and delicious, if you can catch them before they fall to the forest floor or get too mushy. Native Americans ate the young shoots and brewed a tea from the leaves.

Thimbleberry

NORTHERN BEDSTRAW
Galium boreale L.
Madder Family (Rubiaceae)

Northern Bedstraw

Description: Northern bedstraw has numerous erect, square stems, 4–32" tall. The leaves are whorled, with 4 narrow leaves that attach to the stem at the same level. Secondary branches often grow from the axis of the primary leaves, making the plant rather densely leaved. The numerous white flowers are arranged in panicles from the leaf axis of the upper leaves and ends of the branches. Each tiny flower consists of 4 petal lobes, 4 stamens, and 2 styles. The fruit is a dry, 2-parted pod, often covered with short, straight or sometimes curled hair.

June–August.

Habitat/Range: Grasslands, meadows, and open woods from plains and valleys to subalpine forests.

Comments: *Galium* is from the Greek word *gala* (milk); a species of *Galium* was used in Europe for curdling milk. *Boreale* refers to the northern (boreal) home range of the species. The name bedstraw comes from the practice of using the dry foliage for stuffing mattresses and pillows.

CHOKECHERRY
Prunus virginiana L.
Rose Family (Rosaceae)

Chokecherry

Description: The white flowers are arranged in long racemes of 15 or more, on the ends of leafy twigs. Each flower has a superior ovary with a single style, 5 sepals, 5 petals, and about 25 stamens. The fruit is a round, dark purple to black cherry with a single round pit. The leaves are alternately arranged and are egg-shaped to more oval. They have a sharp tip and fine, forward-pointing teeth on the margin. The petiole (leaf stem) has a pair of dark reddish glands just below the base of the leaf blade. The shrubs are alternately branched, up to 24' tall, often forming dense thickets. On dry sites or where heavily browsed they are often much lower (2–6' tall).

May–July.

Habitat/Range: Streams, woody draws; plains, valleys, montane forests.

Comments: Plains Indians pounded the fruit into flat cakes and used the bark to treat diarrhea. Meriwether Lewis, whose mother was an herbalist, used the same treatment successfully on himself when he fell ill below the Great Falls of the Missouri on June 11, 1805. The fresh pits and leaves of chokecherry contain toxic compounds that release cyanide, causing poisoning and death if sufficient quantities are consumed.

Aspen

ASPEN
Populus tremuloides Michx.
Willow Family (Salicaceae)

Description: Aspen is often confused with paper birch. The bark of aspen is smooth and tight, with a greenish white color. Paper birch has chalky white bark that peels in thin paperlike sheets. Aspen has leaves that are rounded or heart-shaped in outline, with vertically flattened petioles (leaf stalks) that are responsible for the distinctive trembling, rotating action in the slightest breeze. The leaves of paper birch are more ovate (egg-shaped), with round petioles, and lack the rotating action of aspen leaves. Both aspen and paper birch have unisexual flowers arranged in catkins. However, aspen is dioecious (with male and female flowers on separate trees), while birch is monoecious (with male and female flowers on the same tree).

Habitat/Range: Montane and subalpine forests.

Comments: Aspen is a colonial tree that spreads vegetatively by shallow underground stems. Patches of aspen trees are often just vertical stems (clones) of a single genetic individual, all connected by a common root system. The borders of the clone patches are often obvious in the spring and fall, when genetic differences in leafing out and fall coloration are expressed between the clone patches. The underground stems enable aspen to survive forest fires with ease. While fire may kill the above ground stems, the buds on the horizontal stems (below ground) are insulated from the heat and quickly resprout. Sucker shoots 6' or more, the first year after a forest fire, are not uncommon. Aspen twigs are a favorite food for browsing deer, elk, and moose, especially in the winter.

Bastard Toad-Flax

BASTARD TOAD-FLAX
Comandra umbellata (L.) Nutt.
Sandalwood Family (Santalaceae)

Description: Bastard toad-flax is a rather in-conspicuous plant, 4–12" tall. The alternate leaves are thick and covered with a whitish substance that gives them a gray-green color. The floral parts are attached to a greenish tube (hypanthium) from the top of the ovary. The flowers have 5 white to purple lobes that extend out from the top of the tube. Each floral lobe has a stamen at the base and a tuft of hairs behind each stamen. The fruit is dry and fleshy with a single seed. Fruit color varies from blue to purple or brown.

April–August.

Habitat/Range: Variety of dry habitats from sea level to subalpine ridges.

Comments: *Comandra* comes from the Greek words *kome* (hair) and *andros* (man), in refer-ence to the tuft of hair behind the stamen, the male part of the flower. These plants are parasitic on a variety of associated plant species. They spread by underground stems and attach them-selves to the roots of other plants. The fruits are reported to be edible, but they may accumulate selenium to toxic levels when growing on soils high in that mineral.

DOTTED SAXIFRAGE
Saxifraga bronchialis L.
Saxifrage Family (Saxifragaceae)

Dotted Saxifrage

Description: The dense clusters of small, rigid, overlapping leaves of dotted saxifrage look like a moss growing in the cracks of boulders and in stony soil. Dainty white flowers, suspended in an open panicle on the slender stems reveal its true identity as a flowering plant. The stems are less than 8" tall, with a few widely spaced, entire (unlobed) leaves. The petals have tiny dots that can be purple, red, or yellow. There are 5 petals, 10 stamens (somewhat shorter than the petals), and 2 styles.

June–September.

Habitat/Range: Rock crevices, rock slides, or scree from sea level to the alpine summits.

Comments: *Saxifraga* is derived from the Latin *saxum* (rock) and *frango* (to break); the plants often grow in rock crevices and appear to be splitting the rock apart. However, the name is thought to have originated, instead, from the herbal use of the plants in Europe to treat urinary stones. *Bronchialis* refers to the bronchial tubes of the lungs of animals, perhaps for the resemblance of the open branching of the flower arrangement to the similar branching of the bronchial tubes.

BROOK SAXIFRAGE
Saxifraga odontoloma Piper
(Also *Saxifraga arguta* D. Don)
Saxifrage Family (Saxifragaceae)

Description: The peculiar basal leaves (mostly round in outline with very coarse teeth) and the habitat (cold, shady streams) are distinctive features of brook saxifrage. Each plant has a single, leafless stem, 8–24" tall, which supports more than 10 flowers in an open panicle arrangement. The small flowers consist of 5 green to purple sepals, 5 round, white petals, 10 stamens with expanded petal-like filaments, and a mostly superior ovary with 2 styles.

May–September.

Habitat/Range: Near water, often on stony stream banks in montane and subalpine forests zones up to timberline.

Comments: *Odontoloma* comes from the Greek roots *odonto* (tooth), and *lomat* (fringe; border), and *arguta* (sharp)—all probably refer to the prominent teeth on the border of the leaves.

Brook Saxifrage

PARROT'S BEAK
Pedicularis racemosa Dougl. ex Benth.
Figwort Family (Scrophulariaceae)

Description: Parrot's beak is named for the long, slender, downturned beak of the galea, or upper lip, of the petals. The lower lip of the petals consists of 2 large lateral lobes and a smaller central lobe. The calyx (sepal) tube has only 2 lobes, while most species of *Pedicularis* in the Central Rocky Mountains have 5 calyx lobes. Parrot's beak has simple leaves with fine, sharp teeth on the margin; most other species in the Central Rocky Mountains have compound leaves, being lobed or divided into many segments. Parrot's beak has leafy stems less than 20" tall.

July–August.

Habitat/Range: Upper montane and subalpine forests.

Comments: There are two varieties of parrot's beak. The variety *alba,* with white flowers, is found east of the Cascade/Sierra crest, including the Central Rocky Mountains. Plants with pink to purple flowers grow west of the summit of the Cascade Range and the Sierra Nevadas.

Parrot's Beak

HOT-ROCK BEARDTONGUE
Penstemon deustus Dougl. ex Lindl.
Figwort Family (Scrophulariaccae)

Description: This white-flowered beardtongue is often seen growing from the rocks in sunny exposures. The leaves usually have coarse, sharp teeth along the margin, especially on the upper portion of the plant. The stems are distinctly woody toward the base. The creamy white petal tube flares into 5 irregular lobes: 2 upper and 3 lower. There are 4 fertile stamens plus a sterile stamen (staminode) that is sparsely bearded, if at all. The staminode just reaches the mouth of the petal tube. Fine glandular hair covers the sepals, the petals (inside and out), and the stems within the flower arrangement.

May–July.

Habitat/Range: Dry, rocky places in the valleys, foothills, and montane and subalpine forests.

Comments: Hot-rock beardtongue is easily distinguished from other white beardtongues by its coarsely toothed leaves, shrubby stems, and its affinity for exposed, rocky habitat. The Shoshone Indians of Nevada referred to this plant as the "bad disease medicine," for its use in treating venereal diseases. The plant was also used medicinally for ear infections, swellings, sore feet, bad eyes, and stomachache.

Hot-Rock Beardtongue

White Beardtongue

WHITE BEARDTONGUE
Penstemon albidus Nutt.
Figwort Family (Scrophulariaceae)

Description: The leaf margin is usually entire, but sometimes there are a few scattered small teeth. The basal leaves are up to 4" long, while the stem leaves are often somewhat smaller. The petal tube flares into 5 irregular lobes: 2 upper and 3 lower. There are 4 fertile stamens plus a sterile stamen (staminode) that is bearded with yellow hair; all are included within the petal tube. Fine glandular hair covers the petals (inside and out) and the stems within the flower arrangement. The stems are herbaceous and up to 20" tall. The white flowers are sometimes tinted pink or bluish.

June–July.

Habitat/Range: Plains and foothills; MT, WY.

Comments: *Penstemon* is said to be derived from the Latin *paene* (nearly) and the Greek *stemon* (thread), which would refer to the sterile stamen (staminode); in this genus, the fifth stamen is not fully developed and thus is "nearly a stamen." Other authors contend that *Penstemon* is derived from the Greek *pente,* meaning "five," and *stemon,* for the 5 stamens (4 fertile and 1 infertile), which are typical of the genus. *Penstemon* includes over 250 species in North America, and is one of the largest genera on the continent.

Edible Tobacco-Root

EDIBLE TOBACCO-ROOT
Valeriana edulis Nutt. ex T. & G.
Valerian Family (Valerianaceae)

Description: The thick taproot of edible to-bacco-root easily distinguishes it from other *Valeriana* species in the Central Rocky Mountains, but please do not dig them up to find out. It is just as easy to identify this plant by looking at the abundant basal leaves. They are simple, widest well above the middle, and taper gradually from there to the narrow base. The opposite leaves on the stems are usually compound, each consisting of many narrow, pinnate segments. The cream-colored flowers are arranged in a panicle. The fruit is a round achene (like a sunflower seed), with plumes on the top for wind dispersal.

June–August.

Habitat/Range: Moist meadows from foothills to alpine summits.

Comments: *Valeriana* was probably named for the Roman province of Valeria, formerly part of Pannonia in southern Europe, now part of Hungary and Croatia. The Tobacco Root Mountains, in the Middle Rockies of Montana, were named for this plant. The Blackfoot Indians called this plant "smell foot" and made a drink from it to treat stomach trouble. The plant was a major food source for other Native Americans; they considered the root poisonous when raw but rendered it safe for eating by baking. It has a very strong and peculiar flavor that is an acquired taste, like Limburger cheese. The odor of the root is equally strong, described by some as smelling like "dirty socks."

GLOSSARY

Alternate—placed singly along a stem or axis, one after another, usually each successive item on a different side from the previous; often used in reference to the arrangement of leaves on a stem (*see* Opposite, illustration p. 16)

Angular—having angles or sharp corners; generally used in reference to stems, as contrasted with round stems.

Annual—a plant completing its life cycle, from seed germination to production of new seeds, within a year and then dying.

Awn—a slender, stiff bristle or fiber attached at its base to another part, such as a leaf tip.

Basal—at the base or bottom of; generally used in reference to leaves.

Biennial—a plant that completes its life cycle in two years; normally not producing flowers during the first year.

Boreal—northern.

Bract—reduced or modified leaf, often associated with flowers.

Bractlet—a small bract.

Bristle—a stiff hair, usually erect or curving away from its attachment point.

Bulb—underground plant part derived from a short, usually rounded shoot that is covered with scales or leaves.

Calyx—the outer set of flower parts, composed of the sepals, which may be separate or joined together; usually green.

Capsule—a dry fruit that releases seeds through splits or holes.

Circumboreal—found around the world at high latitudes or elevations.

Circumpolar—found around the world in alpine or polar regions.

Clasping—Surrounding or partially wrapping around a stem or branch.

Cluster—any grouping or close arrangement of individual flowers that is not dense and continuous.

Compound Leaf—a leaf that is divided into two to many leaflets, each of which may look like a complete leaf but which lacks buds. Compound leaves may have leaflets arranged along an axis like the rays of a feather or radiating from a common point like the fingers on a hand (*see* illustration p. 16).

Conifer—a cone-bearing tree or shrub.

Corm—an enlarged base or stem resembling a bulb.

Corolla—the set of flower parts interior to the calyx and surrounding the stamens, composed of the petals which may be free or united; often brightly colored.

Disk Flower—small, tubular flowers in the central portion of the flower head of many plants in the aster family (Asteraceae)(*see* illustration p. 21).

Disturbed—referring to habitats that have been impacted by actions or processes associated with European settlement such as ditching, grading, or long intervals of high-intensity grazing.

Draw—a small, elongate depression with gentle side slopes in an upland landscape resembling a miniature valley or ravine.

Ecosystem—recognizable community of plants and animals affected by environmental factors such as elevation, wind, temperature, precipitation, sunlight, soil type, and direction of slope.

Entire—a leaf edge that is smooth, without teeth or notches.

Erect—upright, standing vertically or directly perpendicular from a surface.

Escape—referring to plants that have been cultivated in an area and spread from there into the wild.

Family—a group of plants having biologically similar features such as flower anatomy, fruit type, etc.

Fellfield—tundra area comprised greatly of broken rock, possibly interspersed with accumulations of soils and plant life.

Fen—a specialized wetland permanently supplied with mineralized groundwater.

Flower Head—as used in this guide, a dense and continuous group of flowers without obvious branches or space between them; used especially in reference to the aster family (Asteraceae).

Genus—a group of closely related species such as the genus *Viola*, encompassing the violets (*see* Specific Name).

Gland—a bump, projection or round protuberance, usually colored differently than the object on which it occurs, and often sticky or producing sticky or oily secretions.

Herbaceous—fleshy stemmed; not woody.

Hood—curving or folded, petal-like structures interior to the petals and exterior to the stamens in certain flowers, including in milkweeds. Since most milkweeds have bent-back petals, the hoods are typically the most prominent feature of the flowers.

Hooded—arching over and partially concealing or shielding.

Horn—a small, round, or flattened projection from the hoods of milkweed flowers.

Host—as used here, a plant from which a parasitic plant derives nourishment.

Hypanthium—the enlargement of the floral receptacle, bearing on its rim the sepals, petals, and stamen.

Infusion—a tealike beverage made by steeping plant parts (usually leaves) in hot water.

Keel—a sharp, lengthwise fold or ridge, referring particularly to the two fused petals forming the lower lip in many flowers of the bean family (Fabaceae).

Lance-shaped—shaped like the head of a lance or spear.

Leaflet—a distinct, leaflike segment of a compound leaf.

Ligule—a protruding, often scale-like structure at the base of the leaf blade in many grasses and some sedges.

Lobe—a segment of an incompletely divided plant part, typically rounded; often used in reference to leaves.

Margin—the edge of a leaf or petal.

Mat—densely interwoven or tangled, low plant growth.

Mesic—referring to a habitat that is well-drained but generally moist through most of the growing season.

Opposite—paired directly across from one another along a stem or axis (*see* Alternate, illustration p. 16).

Ovary—the portion of the flower where the seeds develop, usually a swollen area below the style (if present) and stigma.

Ovate—egg shaped.

Palmate—spreading like the fingers of a hand (*see* illustration p. 16).

Parallel—side by side, approximately the same distance apart, for the entire length; often used in reference to veins or edges of leaves.

Perennial—a plant that normally lives for three or more years.

Petal—component parts of the corolla, often the most brightly colored and visible parts of the flower.

Pinnate—divided or lobed along each side of a leaf stalk, resembling a feather (*see* illustration p. 16).

Pistil—the seed-producing, or female, unit of a flower, consisting of the ovary, style (if present), and stigma; a flower may have one to several separate pistils.

Pod—a dry fruit that splits open along the edges.

Pollen—tiny, often powdery, male reproductive cells formed in the stamens and typically necessary for seed production.

Prickle—a small, sharp, spine-like outgrowth from the outer surface.

Raceme—unbranched stem with stalked flowers, the newest flowers forming at the top.

Ray—(Apiaceae) the radiating branches of an umbel.

Ray Flower—flower in the aster family (Asteraceae) with a single, strap-shaped corolla resembling one flower petal; ray flowers may surround the disk flowers in a flower head or, in some species such as dandelions, the flower heads may be composed entirely of ray flowers (*see* illustration p. 21).

Resinous—containing or covered with sticky to semisolid, clearish sap or gum.

Rhizomes—underground stems that produce roots and shoots at the nodes.

Rosette—a dense cluster of basal leaves from a common underground part, often in a flattened, circular arrangement (*see* illustration p. 16).

Runner—a long, trailing stem.

Sap—the juice within a plant.

Sedge—a large group of grasslike plants, many of which grow in wetlands.

Seepage—referring to an area with small volumes of subsurface water supply.

Sepal—component part of the calyx; typically green but sometimes enlarged and brightly colored.

Serrate—possessing sharp, forward-pointing teeth.

Shrub—small, multistemmed, woody plant.

Simple Leaf—a leaf that has a single leaflike blade, although this may be lobed or divided (*see* illustration p. 16).

Specific Name—the second portion of a scientific name, identifying a particular species; for instance in Colorado Columbine, *Aquilegia coerula*, the specific name is *coerula*.

Spike—an elongate, unbranched cluster of stalkless or nearly stalkless flowers.

Spine—a thin, stiff, sharp-pointed projection.

Spreading—extending outward from; at right angles to; widely radiating.

Spur—hollow, tubular projection from the base of a petal or sepal; often producing nectar.

Stalk—as used here, the stem supporting the leaf or flower cluster.

Stalkless—lacking a stalk. A stalkless leaf is attached directly to the stem at the leaf base.

Stamen—the male unit of a flower which produces the pollen; typically consisting of a long filament with a pollen-producing tip.

Standard—the usually erect, spreading upper petal in many flowers of the bean family (Fabaceae).

Steppe—arid land with drought tolerant vegetation.

Sterile—in flowers, referring to inability to produce seeds; in habitats, referring to poor nutrient and mineral availability in the soil.

Stigma—portion of the pistil receptive to pollination; usually at the top of the style, and often appearing fuzzy or sticky.

Stipule—bract or leafy structure occurring in pairs at the base of the leaf stalk.

Style—the portion of the pistil between the ovary and the stigma; typically a slender stalk.

Subspecies—a group of plants within a species that has consistent, repeating, genetic and structural distinctions.

Succulent—thickened and fleshy or juicy.

Swale—a depression or shallow hollow in the land, typically moist.

Taproot—a stout, main root extending downward.

Tendril—a slender, coiled, or twisted filament with which climbing plants attach to their support.

Tepal—petals and sepals that cannot be distinguished from each other.

Ternate—arranged in threes, as the leaflets of a compound leaf.

Toothed—bearing teeth or sharply angled projections along the edge.

Trifoliate—having three leaves.

Tuber—thick, creeping underground stems; sometimes also used for thickened portions of roots.

Tubercle—small, rounded projection, as occurs on a cactus or on a plant root.

Tubular—narrow, cylindrical, and tube-like.

Variety—a group of plants within a species that has a distinct range, habitat, or structure.

Veins—bundles of small tubes that carry water, minerals, and nutrients.

Whorl—three or more parts attached at the same point along a stem or axis and often surrounding the stem.

Winged—having thin bands of leaflike tissue attached edgewise along the length.

Wings—the two side petals flanking the keel in many flowers of the bean family (Fabaceae).

Woody—firm-stemmed or branched.

NATIVE PLANT DIRECTORY

To find out more about wildflowers and other plants native to the Central Rockies the reader may wish to contact the native plant societies and natural heritage data centers listed below. The state native plant societies are diverse groups of amateur and professional plant enthusiasts organized to share information about the study and conservation of plants native to their states. The natural heritage data centers maintain comprehensive data bases that list the rare, threatened and endangered plants, animals and ecosystems within their states.

NATIVE PLANT SOCIETIES

Idaho
Idaho Native Plant Society
P.O. Box 9451
Boise, ID 83707-3451

Montana
Montana Native Plant Society
P.O. Box 8783
Missoula, MT 59807-8783

Oregon
Native Plant Society of Oregon
P.O. Box 902
Eugene, OR 97440
Website: www.teleport.com/nonprofit/npso/

Washington
Washington Native Plant Society
P.O. Box 28690
Seattle, WA 98118
Website: www.wnps.org

Wyoming
Wyoming Native Plant Society
1604 Grand Ave. Suite 2
Laramie, WY 82070

NATURAL HERITAGE DATA CENTERS

Idaho
Conservation Data Center
Idaho Department of Fish and Game
600 S. Walnut, P.O. Box 25
Boise, ID 83707-0025
Phone: 208/334-3402
Fax: 208/334-2114
Email: bmoseley@idfg.state.id.us
Website: www2.state.id.us/fishgame/
   cdchome.htm

Montana
Montana Natural Heritage Program
State Library Building
1515 E. 6th Ave.
Helena, MT 59620
Phone: 406/444-3009
Fax: 406/444-0581
Email: mtnhp@nris.state.mt.us
Website: www.nris.gov/mtnhp/

Oregon
Oregon Natural Heritage Program
821 SE 14th Ave.
Portland, OR 97214
Phone: 503/731-3070
Fax: 503/230-9639
Email: svrilakas@tnc.org
Website: www.abi.org/nhp/us/or

Washington
Washington Natural Heritage Program
Department of Natural Resources
P.O. Box 47016
Olympia, WA 98504-7016
Phone: 360/902-1340
Fax: 360/902-1783
Email: john.gamon@wadnr.gov
Website: www.wa.gov/dnr/htdocs/fr/nhp

Wyoming
Wyoming Natural Diversity Database
1604 Grand Avenue, Suite 2
Laramie, WY 82070
Phone: 307/745-5026
Fax: 307/745-1506
Email: wndd@uwyo.edu

SELECTED REFERENCES

Bailey, Robert G. 1995. Description of the Ecoregions of the United States. 2nd ed. USDA Forest Service Misc. Pub. No. 1391, Washington, D.C.

Cronquist, Arthur et al. 1986–1997. *Intermountain Flora* (vols. 1, 3A, 3B, 4, 5, and 6). The New York Botanical Garden, New York, NY.

Davis, Ray J. 1952. *Flora of Idaho*. Wm. C. Brown Co., Dubuque, IA.

Dorn, Robert D. 1984. *Vascular Plants of Montana*. Mountain West Publishing, Cheyenne, WY.

Dorn, Robert D. 1992. *Vascular Plants of Wyoming*. Mountain West Publishing, Cheyenne, WY.

Dowden, Anne Ophelia. 1978. *State Flowers*. Thomas Y. Crowell, New York, NY.

Featherly, H. I. 1965. *Taxonomic Terminology of the Higher Plants*. Hafner Publishing Company, Inc., New York, NY.

Furman, T. E. and J. M. Trappe. 1971. "Phylogeny and Ecology of Mycotropic Achlorophyllous Angiosperms." *Quarterly Review of Biology* 46: 219–225.

Gilmore, Melvin R. 1919. "Uses of Plants by the Indians of the Missouri River Region." *Thirty-third Annual Report of the Bureau of American Ethnology*. U.S. Government Printing Office, Washington, D.C. Reproduced 1977, University of Nebraska Press, Lincoln, NE.

Great Plains Flora Association. 1986. *Flora of the Great Plains*. University Press of Kansas, Lawrence, KS.

Haines, Aubrey L. 1977. *The Yellowstone Story: A History of Our First National Park*. Yellowstone Library and Museum Association, Yellowstone National Park, WY.

Harrington, H. D. 1967. *Edible Native Plants of the Rocky Mountains*. The University of New Mexico Press, Albuquerque, NM.

Hart, Jeff. 1976. *Montana—Native Plants and Early Peoples*. Montana Historical Society, Helena, MT.

Hitchcock, C. Leo and Arthur Cronquist. 1973. *Flora of the Pacific Northwest*. University of Washington Press, Seattle, WA.

Hitchcock, C. Leo; Arthur Cronquist; Marion Ownbey; and J. W. Thompson. 1955–1969. *Vascular Plants of the Pacific Northwest* (vols. 1–5). University of Washington Press, Seattle, WA.

Hoffmann, David. 1983. *The Holistic Herbal*. The Findhorn Press, The Park, Forres, Scotland.

Hopkins, A.D. 1938. *Bioclimatics: A Science of Life and Climatic Relations*. U.S. Department of Agriculture Miscellaneous Publication 280: 1–188.

Inouye, D. W. and O. R. Taylor, Jr. 1980. "Variation in Generation Time in Frasera Speciosa (Gentianaceae), a Long-lived Perennial Monocarp." *Oecologia* 47: 171–174.

Inouye, D. W. 1984. "The Ant and the Sunflower." *Natural History* June: 49–52.

Johnston, Alex. 1987. *Plants and the Blackfoot.* Lethbridge Historical Society, City of Lethbridge, Lethbridge, Alberta.

Kindscher, Kelly. 1992. *Medicinal Wild Plants of the Prairie.* University Press of Kansas, Lawrence, KS.

Kingsbury, John M. 1964. *Poisonous Plants of the United States and Canada.* Prentice-Hall, Inc., Englewood Cliffs, NJ.

Lackschewitz, Klaus. 1986. *Plants of West-Central Montana—Identification and Ecology: Annotated Checklist.* USDA Forest Service General Technical Report INT-217, Ogden, UT.

Lesica, P. and D. Hanna. 1996. *Vascular Plants of Pine Butte Swamp Preserve: An Annotated Checklist.* The Nature Conservancy, Helena, MT.

Lewis, Walter H. and Memory P. F. Elvin-Lewis. 1977. *Medical Botany: Plants Affecting Man's Health.* John Wiley & Sons, Inc., New York, NY.

Moore, Michael. 1979. *Medicinal Plants of the Mountain West.* The Museum of New Mexico Press, Santa Fe, NM.

Morin, Nancy R., ed. 1993–97. *Flora of North America* (vols. 1, 2, and 3). Oxford University Press, Oxford.

Ody, Penelope. 1993. *The Complete Medicinal Herbal.* Dorling Kindersley Limited, London.

Porter, C. L. 1959. *Taxonomy of Flowering Plants.* W. H. Freeman and Co., Inc., San Francisco, CA.

Reese, Rick. 1981. *Montana Mountain Ranges.* Montana Magazine, Inc., Helena, MT.

Reese, Rick. 1991. *Greater Yellowstone: The National Park and Adjacent Wildlands.* American and World Geographic Publishing, Helena, MT.

Shaw, Richard J. 1992. *Annotated Checklist of the Vascular Plants of Grand Teton National Park and Teton County, Wyoming.* Grand Teton Natural History Association, Moose, WY.

Strickler, Dee; Zoe Strickler; and Anne Morley. 1997. *Northwest Penstemons.* Flower Press, Columbia Falls, MT.

Train, Percy; James R. Henrichs; and W. Andrew Archer. 1957. *Contributions toward a Flora of Nevada, No. 45, Medicinal Uses of Plants by Indian Tribes of Nevada.* USDA Agricultural Research Service, Beltsville, MD.

Williams, Kim. 1984. *Eating Wild Plants.* Mountain Press Publishing Co., Missoula, MT.

Wuerthner, George. 1986. *Idaho Mountain Ranges.* American Geographic Publishing, Helena, MT.

Zwinger, Ann H. and Beatrice E. Willard. 1972. *Land above the Trees.* Harper & Row, New York, NY.

INDEX OF FAMILY NAMES

INDEX OF PLANT NAMES

About the Author

H. Wayne Phillips, formerly a Forest Service ecologist, range manager, and forester is now devoting his full time to teaching and writing about the flora of the Rocky Mountains and Great Plains. He has taught botany/wildflower classes at the Yellowstone Institute for fifteen years. His teaching experience also includes botany classes as a faculty affiliate at the University of Montana, Montana State University-Northern and the Univer-

sity of Great Falls. He is currently the president of the Montana Native Plant Society. His hobbies include ethnobotany, herbalism, wildflower photography, canoeing, and mountaineering. Wayne's current, on-going botanical studies include collecting and photographing all of the plant species that were collected and described by Meriwether Lewis in 1804-1806. He is contributing this collection to the Lewis and Clark Expedition Interpretive Center, near his home in Great Falls, Montana.